D0806053

3-21

THE
MILITANT
BLACK
WRITER

THE
MILITANT
BLACK
WRITER

IN AFRICA
AND THE
UNITED
STATES

Mercer Cook *and*
Stephen E. Henderson

THE UNIVERSITY OF WISCONSIN PRESS
Madison, Milwaukee, and London, 1969

Published by
The University of Wisconsin Press
Box 1379, Madison, Wisconsin 53701
The University of Wisconsin Press, Ltd.
27-29 Whitfield Street, London, W.1

Copyright © 1969 by the Regents of
The University of Wisconsin
All rights reserved

Second printing, 1969

Printed in the United States of America
SBN 299–05391–1, paper 299–05394–6; LC 69–17324

Foreword

THE two essays that make up this volume were originally delivered in shorter form as papers at the first meeting of a two-day symposium, " 'Anger, and Beyond': The Black Writer and a World in Revolution," held in Madison, Wisconsin, on August 8 and 9, 1968.

The idea of such a symposium was conceived by William A. Brown, a black graduate student in the Department of History at the University of Wisconsin, who in May of 1968 had brilliantly and almost single-handedly put together a notable Madison Conference on Afro-American Letters and Arts, and had led in the organization of the Wisconsin Academy of African-American Letters and Arts. Upon his urging of a symposium on the militant black writer, the Department of English agreed to be sponsor; and accordingly a steering committee was formed consisting of Mr. Brown and two departmental representatives, Professor Jerome J. Donnelly and the writer of this Foreword, who was then chairman of the Department. In organizing the event this committee functioned easily as a triumvirate without a chairman. Had a chairman been necessary, it should have been William Brown, who worked at his share of the task with impressive imagination and energy while at the same time calmly carrying on research for his doctoral dissertation in African Studies.

81225

It was Mr. Brown who suggested Mercer Cook and
Stephen Henderson as the participants in the symposium's
first meeting. The suggestion was an excellent one. Professor Mercer Cook, head of the Department of Romance
Languages at Howard University, is in the midst of a
distinguished career as teacher, scholar, author, translator,
and diplomat. Professor Stephen E. Henderson is chairman
of the Department of English at Morehouse College, is a
poet and essayist, and has published articles on the relationship between Negro folk poetry and jazz. Equally skilled
and utterly different as lecturers, they made on the plat-
form an exciting contrast of persons and approaches: Cook,
the older man, tall, slender, learned, witty, seemingly detached but deeply committed; Henderson, the younger
man, short, stocky, intense, communicating as much by the
highly personal insight of the poet as by analytic argument;
but both men gifted with the talent for the memorable
phrase and each in his way saying things that needed to be
heard.

As a reading of the expanded versions of their papers will
show, Cook and Henderson differ in their subject matters
and in their attitudes, scholarly and personal, toward them.
Cook outlines a tradition of protest among African poets
and novelists of the last half-century, a tradition prefigured,
as he points out, in the acts and writings of African journalists, lawyers, and preachers of the half-century preceding
this past one; and, sympathetic but judicious, he concludes
that "In the main, statements by the Africans seem to me
less extreme and violent than many by West Indian and
North American blacks." Henderson, on the other hand,
deals primarily with the black writers and jazz artists, but
particularly with the poets, who in the present-day United
States are concerned with creating what he calls "Black

Consciousness"; and his tone, perhaps because he is one of these poets himself, is far less detached and much more intransigeant than that of his fellow scholar. Yet despite their differences these two men are in important ways talking about remarkably similar elements in the literary expression of the black African and the black American experiences, and the "key words" used by Cook both to organize his survey of militant African literature and to express its central themes closely parallel the key concepts used by Henderson to give his readers some sense of what is going on in American black writing today. Three of these key words or concepts should be noted.

Whether he is African or American by place of birth, the black writer by the conditions of his existence has been made intensely aware of a white "civilization," which, whatever its virtues, nevertheless does impose its domination on the black body and mind. This domination may be of the openly oppressive sort, such as the jailing of black leaders or the socio-economic imprisonment of black people in ghettos, or it may be of the covert sort whereby values accepted by whites are invoked by them in opposition to important black values of which whites are ignorant. Thus Cook notes that for the African authors he discusses white "civilization" meant ambivalently "education and exploitation, hospitals and haughtiness, Christianity and segregated churches, money and misery, knowledge but not wisdom, progress but not partnership." Henderson, who is more concerned with the vices of white "civilization" than any virtues, asserts that the United States "has been built upon violence, physical, mental, and spiritual— by the virtual extermination of the Indian, by the enslavement of the African and the systematic degradation of his progeny in America." More broadly, he argues, because of their "equation of blackness and evil" it can be said that "Western religion, Western iconography, Western symbolism, all conspire to create black self-hatred, black self-denial, black slavery."

Just as both the African and the American black writer attack white "civilization," so both emphasize the black person's search for identity. Cook describes the impact of this search on the African writer: "Taking the white man's language, dislocating his syntax, recharging his words with new strength and sometimes with new meaning before hurling them back in his teeth, while upsetting his self-righteous complacency and clichés, our poets rehabilitate such terms as Africa and blackness, beauty and peace." Henderson, declaring that "Our poets are now our prophets," writes that these poets "come to baptize us in blackness," to affirm "black selfhood." Such an affirmation, he points out, is made by the protagonist of Ralph Ellison's extraordinary novel, *Invisible Man*, when in a famous scene the "nameless hero" confronts and accepts his blackness by eating a baked yam openly on the street. ("I yam what I am!" Ellison has his hero say exuberantly, the act of punning, a form of linguistic liberation, expressing and corresponding to his psychological liberation.)

Finally, the African and the American black writers are similar in their attempts to define and to give content to a special term, *negritude* or *African personality* for the African, *soul* for the American. Despite the recognized differences between these terms, each represents a negative reaction against the domination of white "civilization" and a positive action toward identity. Each asserts special aspects of black African or black American experience that are qualitatively different from white experience. Each term, as Cook and Henderson see it, represents a rejection of a set of values—white, usually middle class—that assume the goodness of the machine and of the rationalistic response to life. So Cook quotes the South African Ezekiel Mphahlele on the white man and his achievements: "He may teach me how to make a shirt or to read and write, but my forebears and I could teach him a thing or two if only he would listen and allow himself time to feel." And Henderson, stating flatly that "Soul is a black man's thing," quotes and amplifies Lerone Bennett's definition of the American term: "*Soul* is a metaphorical evocation of Negro being as expressed in the Negro tradition. It is the feeling with which an artist invests his creation, the style with which a man lives his life. It is, above all, the spirit rather than the letter: a certain way of feeling, a certain way of expressing oneself, a certain way of being."

The reader, black or white, may or may not agree with every aspect of these two extremely interesting essays, but he would do well first to examine each carefully and sympathetically. Particularly is it important that the white reader of these essays "listen," in Mphahlele's words, "and allow himself time to feel"—listen, really listen, that is, to what Professors Cook and Henderson and the many black writers they aptly quote are saying; not what the white reader thinks they are saying or what he wants them to say, but what in fact they do say. Such listening may not be easy at every point; it will require a willing suspension of fixed belief, an effort toward empathy, an effort perhaps all the greater as we naively assume we can achieve empathy without effort. To the degree that the white reader does listen, however, he will realize that these papers are very much worth being listened to.

In the course of organizing the symposium, " 'Anger, and Beyond': The Black Writer and a World in Revolution," the steering committee incurred debts to many persons and parts of the University of Wisconsin that should here be gratefully acknowledged. Financial support was generously provided by the University Lectures Committee, Dean Leon D. Epstein of the College of Letters and Science, and Acting Chancellor Bryant E. Kearl. Assistance with the arrangements came from the Wisconsin Memorial Union—Mrs. G. N. Musser, Mrs. Rita Peterson, and the Union Literary Committee were especially helpful—from the Wisconsin State Historical Society, from James Collins of WHA Radio, from Robert A. Smithey, and from the sometimes hard-pressed secretaries of the Department of English, particularly Mrs. Nancy Pellmann. Despite the many demands on his time, Samuel D. Proctor, Dean of Special Projects at the University, presided, very ably, over the opening meeting of the symposium.

In addition to the first meeting, the symposium's public meetings included a remarkable poetry reading by Don L. Lee, the young black poet from Chicago, who is quoted in Stephen Henderson's essay, and a memorable round table discussion centering on the black writer, his audience, and his critics, the participants being, in addition to Mr. Lee and the authors of these two papers, Professor Edward L. Kamarck, editor of *Arts in Society;* Professor Joel Roache of the Department of English; and Mr. Leslie Fishel, Director of the Wisconsin State Historical Society. They, too, along with a serious and articulate audience at all the meetings, helped greatly to make the symposium a successful act of cooperation among faculty and students, university and community, whites and blacks.

WALTER B. RIDEOUT

Madison, Wisconsin
December, 1968

Contents

Acknowledgments

For permission to quote from previously published material, acknowledgment is made to the following authors or publishers:

Lebert Bethune, for "Apollo at the Apollo."

Broadside Press, for "Malcolm X," by Gwendolyn Brooks, and "For Brother Malcolm," by Edward Spriggs.

Sterling Brown, for "Ma Rainey."

Harold Courlander, for "Black Woman," as sung by Rich Amerson.

Waring Cuney, for "No Images."

Frank Marshall Davis, for "Robert Whitmore."

Editions CLE, for "Civilisation," by René Philombe.

Mari Evans, for "Black Jam for Dr. Negro," and "Vive Noir!"

Donald Graham, for "Black Song."

Ahmed Le Graham Alhamsi, for "The Black Narrator."

Carl Wendell Hines, Jr., for "Two Jazz Poems."

Indiana University Press, for "Africa's Plea," by Roland Tombekai Dempster; "The Continent That Lies within Us," by Davidson Nicol; "Once upon a Time," by Gabriel Okara. Copyright © 1963 by Langston Hughes.

LeRoi Jones, for "Poem for Black Hearts."

Alfred A. Knopf, for excerpt from "Jazzonia," by Langston Hughes. Copyright © 1926 by Alfred A. Knopf, Inc.; renewed 1954 by Langston Hughes.

Don L. Lee, for "In the Interest of Black Salvation."

The Liberator, for "to/blk/record/buyers," by Sonia Sanchez.

Laurence Neal and *Negro Digest*, for "Don't Say Goodbye to the Pork-Pie Hat."

Negro Digest, for "Point of Departure," by William Kgositsile, and "For All Things Black and Beautiful," by Conrad Kent Rivers.

Le Niger, for "Lapsus," by Bania Mahamadou Say.

Phelps Stokes Fund, for "The Parable of the Eagle," by J. E. K. Aggrey.

Présence Africaine, for "Sur le tombeau de John Kennedy," by Lamine Diakhaté; "Blues," by Assane Diallo; "Le Temps du martyre," by David Diop.

Léopold Sédar Senghor, for "Chaka," "New York," and "Prayer for Peace."

Viking Press, for "Black and Unknown Bards," by James Weldon Johnson. Copyright © 1917 by James Weldon Johnson.

Yale University Press, for "For My People," by Margaret Walker. Copyright © 1942 by Yale University Press.

African Voices
of Protest

MERCER COOK

THE three revolutionary quotations that I open with may be familiar to most readers. All three statements were originally made in French. The first deals directly with literature:

"What did you expect when you removed the gag that closed those black mouths? That they would sing your praises? Those heads that our fathers pressed to the ground, did you expect to read adoration in their eyes when they could look up?"[1]

The second is somewhat psychological: "The less intelligent the white man is, the more stupid the black man seems to him."[2]

And the third, political, economic, and social, translates thus: "If I were chief of one of the African peoples, I declare that I would have a gallows set up at the frontier, on which I would hang, without mercy, the first European who dared enter the country, and the first citizen who tried to leave it."[3]

You have probably recognized quotation number one, as the beginning of Jean-Paul Sartre's famous preface to Léo-

1. J.-P. Sartre, in his preface to Senghor's *Anthologie de la nouvelle poésie nègre et malgache*, p. ix. (All translations from French in this essay are my own, unless otherwise credited.)
2. André Gide, *Voyage au Congo*, p. 21.
3. J.-J. Rousseau, *Oeuvres complètes* (Paris, 1823), I, 152.

pold Sédar Senghor's 1948 anthology. Quotation number two, equally famous, comes from André Gide's account of his trip to the Congo in 1926. The third goes all the way back to the mid-eighteenth century, to a letter written by Jean-Jacques Rousseau. I have selected those passages more or less at random as a reminder at the outset of this discussion that the African has had powerful allies in his struggle for freedom, equality, and dignity, and that the written protest did not begin yesterday. As early as 1808 the Abbé Henri Grégoire, in his *De la Littérature des Nègres*, was able to list more than two hundred Europeans among the "courageous men who have pleaded the cause of the unfortunate blacks and mixed bloods." In the same dedication, Grégoire included eight Negroes.[4] Their numbers would soon increase and so, eventually, would their militancy, though it would hardly equal in violence the cry of the Haitian revolutionary: "Coupez têtes, brûlez cailles" (Chop off heads, burn down huts).

Like the Haitians and their abolitionist friends, most of the early African writers directed their appeal for justice to the humanitarian, Christian conscience of the European, while stimulating in their compatriots a sense of self-respect

4. These were Anthony William Amo, a scholar from the Gold Coast (now Ghana), trained in European universities, and one-time professor at Wittenburg; Ottobah Cugoana, former slave, author of *Thoughts and Sentiments on the evil and wicked traffic of the Slavery and Commerce of the human species* (London, 1787); Othello, who published in Baltimore an essay against slavery in 1788; Ignatius Sancho, former slave, author of two volumes of letters (London, 1782); Gustavus Vassa, also a former slave, who wrote an autobiography; poets Phillis Wheatley and Milscent, the former from Senegal, the latter from Haiti; and Julien Raimond, wealthy mulatto from Saint-Domingue (later Haiti), author of numerous brochures, subsequently a collaborator of Toussaint-Louverture.

and solidarity, a desire for education, progress, and self-government. For an introduction to these pioneer authors, I would recommend Robert W. July's *The Origins of Modern African Thought*, especially the chapters on Edward W. Blyden, Thomas Horatio Jackson, J. E. Casely Hayford, Bishop James Johnson, and "Reversible" Johnson. Blyden, whom July calls "the first African personality," was, among other things, a precursor of negritude, a concept to be discussed shortly. As early as 1880 he felt that "Africa may yet prove to be the spiritual conservatory of the world," as the rest of humanity becomes mired in materialism. "I would rather be a member of this race," he proudly contended, "than a Greek in the time of Alexander, a Roman in the Augustan period, or an Anglo-Saxon in the nineteenth century" (July, p. 218).

Anticipating a movement that would reach the United States decades later, several of these men adopted African names: the Reverend Samuel Richard Drew Solomon, grandson of a former king in the Gold Coast, changed his name to Attoh Ahuma. George W. Johnson opted for Osokele Tejumade Johnson, explaining that "George W." was "a foreign and a slave name"—but they still called him "Reversible." Bishop James Johnson "began arbitrarily to baptize babies with African names, ignoring the wishes and protests of his congregation . . ." (July, p. 287).

Carrying the defense of African culture one step further, nationalist Attoh Ahuma is quoted by July (p. 343) as having written the following in 1905:

We have fought valiantly for what we deemed were our ancestral rights in the past, and would fight again, if those rights were menaced tomorrow—but the greatest calamity of West Africa that must be combated tooth and nail . . . is the

imminent loss of ourselves. . . . Rather let men rob our lands
. . . but let us see that they do not rob us of ourselves. They
do so when we are taught to despise our own names, institutions, customs and laws.

By 1896 another distinguished citizen of the Gold Coast,
J. E. Casely Hayford, had envisioned the ideal of African
unity, or at least of West African unity: "Has the reader
ever tried to picture to himself a united West Africa, and
what it would mean? . . . It is a grand idea. The present
age is too feeble to take it in. But it looms large in the
future nevertheless. It may not be in our time. But that it is
realizable is within the region of practical politics" (July, p.
444). By 1920 Casely Hayford had made a start, with the
first National Congress of British West Africa, represent-
ing Nigeria, Sierra Leone, the Gold Coast, and little Gam-
bia as well.

Planting seed that would sprout in a later generation,
these older writers, though less militant than their descendants, none the less spoke up to their colonial overlords.
Witness "Reversible" Johnson formally renouncing British
citizenship, espousing "the idea of Egba nationhood, national independence and territorial integrity" (July, p.
207), adopting the slogan "Africa shall rise," warning the
British that it would take more than missionaries and gun-
boats "to civilize and Christianize Africans," and proposing
"the forming of a proper government among educated
Africans" (July, p. 200). Or read Thomas H. Jackson's
condemnation of Governor Lugard's administration: "For
six long years, we have lived under the cramped condition
of a military dictatorship when the law from being a means
of protection had become an instrument of crime and oppression in the hands of unscrupulous officials. . . . The last

administration has made the very name of the white man stink in the nostrils of the native" (July, p. 364).

These men helped to pave the way for the ardent nationalists who were to follow. How right Nkrumah was to pay tribute to them on March 6, 1957, when Ghana became independent! "Here today the work of Rousseau, the work of Marcus Garvey, the work of Aggrey, the work of Casely Hayford, the work of these illustrious men who have gone before us has come to reality at this present moment" (*I Speak of Freedom*, p. 107).

One of the precursors to whom he referred was Dr. J. E. K. Aggrey, his former teacher, the famous African educator and pastor, whose major contribution to the young Africans of his day was perhaps his insistence on self-reliance and self-respect, his conviction that his racial brethren should raise their sights. This he exemplified in his life and in his lectures to black students here and in Africa, especially in his celebrated "Parable of the Eagle":

A certain man went through a forest seeking any bird of interest he might find. He caught a young eagle, brought it home and put it among his fowls and ducks and turkeys, and gave it chickens' food to eat even though it was an eagle, the king of birds.

Five years later a naturalist came to see him and, after passing through his garden, said: "That bird is an eagle, not a chicken."

"Yes," said its owner, "but I have trained it to be a chicken. It is no longer an eagle, it is a chicken even though it measures fifteen feet from tip to tip of its wings."

"No," said the naturalist, "it is an eagle still; it has the heart of an eagle, and I will make it soar high up to the heavens."

"No," said the owner, "it is a chicken and it will never fly."

They agreed to test it. The naturalist picked up the eagle, held it up, and said with great intensity: "Eagle, thou art an eagle; thou dost belong to the sky and not to this earth; stretch forth thy wings and fly."

The eagle turned this way and that, and then, looking down, saw the chickens eating their food, and down he jumped.

The owner said: "I told you it was a chicken."

"No," said the naturalist, "it is an eagle. Give it another chance to-morrow."

So the next day he took it to the top of the house and said: "Eagle, thou art an eagle; stretch forth thy wings and fly." But again the eagle, seeing the chickens feeding, jumped down and fed with them.

Then the owner said: "I told you it was a chicken."

"No," asserted the naturalist, "it is an eagle, and it still has the heart of an eagle; only give it one more chance, and I will make it fly to-morrow."

The next morning he rose early and took the eagle outside the city, away from the houses, to the foot of a high mountain. The sun was just rising, gilding the top of the mountain with gold, and every crag was glistening in the joy of that beautiful morning.

He picked up the eagle and said to it: "Eagle, thou art an eagle; thou dost belong to the sky and not to this earth; stretch forth thy wings and fly!"

The eagle looked around and trembled as if new life were coming to it; but it did not fly. The naturalist then made it look straight at the sun. Suddenly it stretched out its wings and, with the screech of an eagle, it mounted higher and higher and never returned. It was an eagle, though it had been kept and tamed as a chicken!

My people of Africa, we were created in the image of God, but men have made us think that we are chickens, and we still think we are; but we are eagles. Stretch forth your wings and fly! Don't be content with the food of chickens.[5]

Still another source of nationalism was the African Church. This would not be the first time that Africans and their descendants would use religion in their struggle for freedom. The Haitian insurrection of 1791 allegedly began at a Voodoo ceremony; and, in our own Southland, spirituals such as "Go down, Moses" and "Joshua fit de battle" were less innocuous and "Bibleistic"[6] than Ol' Massa believed. Similarly a Kikuyu suggests that certain sermons had special meanings in colonized Kenya: Daniel in the lion's den, the Hebrew children in the fiery furnace, Balaam's ass. "When the preacher repeated the words of the donkey: 'Why do you beat me so hard?' I am sure now that it had some meanings that Balaam's ass did not put into it."[7] In 1960, Aimé Césaire told a conference in Rome: "One perceives that animist religions have sometimes been the first forms of the anti-colonial struggle. In the Congo, for instance, it is clear that the first anti-colonialists drew treasures of vitality from belonging to a religion different from that of the colonizer."[8] A separatist church appeared

5. Edwin W. Smith, *Aggrey of Africa* (New York: Doubleday, Doran, 1929), pp. 136-137.

6. The term "Bibleistic" was used by Paul Laurence Dunbar in his poem, "An Ante-Bellum Sermon." After telling the slaves how Moses had led the Hebrews out of bondage, the preacher, becoming wary, interrupts his homily:

> But I think it would be bettah,
> Ef I pause agin to say
> Dat I'm talkin' 'bout ouah freedom
> In a Bibleistic way.

7. Gatheru, *Child of Two Worlds*, p. 40.

8. *Comprendre*, No. 21-22 (Venice, 1960; special issue on a joint meeting between the African and European Societies of Culture), p. 232.

in South Africa in 1882; the number of such churches had reached 272 half a century later. In 1891, Blyden had advocated "religious independence for West Africa from the Christian churches of Europe" (July, p. 231). This movement spread, ushering in "prophets and priests" with a brand of Christianity that would, like the spirituals, identify Europeans with Pharaohs and Philistines; the five wise virgins would be black; the five foolish virgins, white.[9] Thomas Hodgkin quotes in French one of the militant hymns of the Kimbanguists. Here it is in English translation:

> Jesus, Savior of the Chosen and Savior of us all,
> We shall be the victors, sent by your call.
> The kingdom is ours. We have it for sure.
> As for the whites, they have it no more.

Even more serious, from the standpoint of the colonialist, was the frequent refusal of these congregations to obey the white man's orders, their rejection of things European, their retention of certain animistic practices. So the colonizer reacted as usual by providing them with martyrs: Mwana Lesa, hanged in Rhodesia in 1926; Simon Kimbangu, condemned to death in 1921 and dying in an Elizabethville prison twenty-nine years later; André Matswa, dying in jail in 1942. In Hodgkin's words: "At least the prophets have awakened men's minds to the fact that change can occur; and the ablest of them . . . have shown themselves wholly capable of constructing a myth, a literature, and an organization" (p. 111).

In addition, the early group of journalists, lawyers, and preachers produced glowing accounts of Africa's past and

9. Cf. Thomas Hodgkin, *Nationalism in Colonial Africa*, p. 97. The hymn that I translate here is on p. 111.

optimistic forecasts of a future in freedom. A new era, combining modern scholarship, militancy, and the authentic voice of African humanism, began in the 1930's. This was a most productive period, culminating in 1938 with the publication of Jomo Kenyatta's *Facing Mount Kenya*. During the previous year Nnamdi Azikiwe brought out his *Renascent Africa,* and Léon G. Damas's *Pigments* appeared in Paris. The following year Aimé Césaire's *Cahier d'un retour au pays natal* and Senghor's "Ce que l'homme noir apporte" were published. These were the years when negritude was discovered in Paris by French-speaking African students, led by Senghor of Senegal, Césaire of Martinique, and Damas of French Guiana. Senghor, the theoretician of negritude, has defined it as "the sum total of cultural values of the Negro world."

As Senghor's friend, I am often asked to define negritude. One of the best answers I know is Samuel W. Allen's: "Negritude, it seems to me, is essentially a means toward the achievement of a sense of full cultural identity and a normal self-pride in the cultural context."[10] Henceforth, whenever I am in a hurry, I will simply borrow "Soul" from Stephen Henderson.[11] This is particularly appropriate. In "Ce que l'homme noir apporte" (p. 313), Senghor stated:

This is a matter of style above all, of soul. . . . However "faithful" the interpretation of great artists like Roland Hayes

10. "Negritude and Its Relevance to the American Negro Writer," in *The American Negro Writer and His Roots,* p. 14.

11. Cf. an article, "African Negritude-Black American Soul," by W. A. Jeanpierre, in *Africa Today,* Vol. 14, No. 6 (December 1967), pp. 10-11: "'Soul' seems to be African Negritude dressed in American clothing, imbuing with an African-American hue all the encounters which have fallen within the province of black-lived experience in America."

or Marian Anderson, something of the negroid interpretation always remains. That special way of surrounding the note, the sound, with a halo of flesh and blood which makes it seem so troubled and so troubling; that "naive" manner of translating the most hidden spirituality by the most earthy voice.

Sometimes, to illustrate negritude, I quote two lines of poetry. The first is from a poem written by a Haitian, Massillon Coicou, in the early 1900's: "Why then am I a Negro? Oh! Why am I black?" The second is by an Ivory Coast poet and novelist, Bernard Dadié, in the early 1950's: "Thank you, Lord, for having made me black."

In the second poem, the inferiority complex based on color has disappeared. After centuries of brainwashing with stereotypes raining down from white lips accusing black folk of innate laziness, dishonesty, stupidity, savagery, and ugliness, one of the main aims of negritude was to inculcate a sense of race pride, respect for the African heritage and potential. In their contacts, literary or personal, with congeners from other lands, the pioneers of negritude discovered not only a common background of suffering, but also a certain similarity of emotional and artistic characteristics: rhythm, humor, intuition, forceful imagery. Speaking at Howard University on September 28, 1966, Senghor paid tribute to "the pioneer thinkers who lighted our road in the years 1930–1935: Alain Locke, W. E. B. DuBois, Marcus Garvey, Carter G. Woodson. And [I should also like] to render well-deserved homage to the poets whom we translated and recited, and in whose steps we tried to follow: Claude McKay, Jean Toomer, Countee Cullen, James Weldon Johnson, Langston Hughes, Sterling Brown." Similar inspiration also came from West Indian writers: from the

Cuban poet Nicolas Guillén, and from Dr. Jean Price-Mars (who has been called "the father of negritude"), Jacques Roumain, and Jean F. Brierre, to name but a few of those who contributed to the Renaissance of Haitian letters.[12]

Along with the transatlantic influence, negritude's three godfathers found much in Europe during the thirties to strengthen their case. In the ethnologists Frobenius, Delafosse, and Griaule, they discovered new reasons for respecting African traditions. Looking back in 1949, Senghor credited Frobenius with enrolling "us in a new *Sturm und Drang* [and leading] us to Wolfgang Goethe. . . . In the footsteps of the Rebel, we revolted against the order and values of the West, especially against its reason." And Aimé Césaire, in his blistering *Discours sur le colonialisme*, published by Présence Africaine in 1955, quoted a passage in which Frobenius called the Africans "civilized to the marrow of their bones. The idea of the barbaric Negro is a European invention" (p. 36). In contemporary painting, sculpture, music, and poetry, the young founders of negritude saw the great modern European artists—Picasso, Matisse, Cézanne, Gauguin, Vlaminck, Stravinsky, Debussy, Dvorak, Rimbaud, and Apollinaire—find inspiration in African art.[13] In Afro-American jazz, in the Brazilian *samba* and the Cuban *son*, they heard the rhythms of their home-

12. Cf. Naomi M. Garrett, *The Renaissance of Haitian Poetry* (Paris: Présence Africaine, 1963).

13. Cf. Senghor's "Ce que l'homme noir apporte," p. 310: "They [modern composers] felt the need to liberate themselves from conventional rules that had become sterile, men like Claude Debussy, Darius Milhaud, and Igor Stravinsky. And they set out to discover unknown alluvions and 'invisible germs.' Responding to these needs is Negro music, which is just beginning to be seriously studied in Europe."

land. Contrasting this European vogue with European attitudes in the colonies, they became convinced that white
was not always right and that black could be beautiful.

> Bare woman, black woman
> Clad in your color which is life, in your form which is
>   beauty

—so sang Senghor, defying the Hollywoodian aesthetic,
while the world applauded and the African woman regally
adjusted her boubou and walked with renewed assurance.

Meanwhile, L. G. Damas, the first of the three forerun-
ners to publish a volume of verse, startled us with *Pigments*,
ridiculing blacks who imitate whites down to "shoes, tux-
edo, dickie, stiff collar, monocle, and derby"; demanding
"black dolls"; equating such racists as "Uncle Gobineau"
and "Cousin Hitler" with "the good Aryan gumming away
his old age on a park bench"; boldly urging the African to
keep out of the white man's war, suggesting that Senegalese
veterans should forget about the "Boches" and "begin by
invading Senegal."

When that was written, World War II, pregnant with
possibilities of colonial liberation, was but two years away.
Thousands of Africans—166,000 with the British, 141,000
with the French, according to the 1956 revision of Lord
Hailey's *An African Survey*—served abroad and witnessed
that crowning example of man's inhumanity to man.

In the process the African soldier learned that the European
was vulnerable—that rifles and large-scale organization were
extraordinary equalizers and that Asian peasants in many in-
stances were even poorer than Africans. These legacies of
World War II were carried back to Africa and the relationship
of white, black, and brown men was never to be the same

again. As surely as the Four Freedoms contributed to a weakening of colonial bonds, the war-time experience of thousands of African youth created a mentality that black men should and could sever these bonds.[14]

Those who remained at home, in Dakar for example, experienced Nazi-dictated discriminatory policies as practiced by the Vichy officials. In January 1944, De Gaulle's Provisional Government held a conference at Brazzaville which promised some liberalization of colonial policy but ruled out "any idea of autonomy, any possibility of evolution outside of the French Empire," as well as "the eventual, even far-distant introduction of self-government." One year later, men like Kenyatta, DuBois, Nkrumah, and Padmore convened the Fifth Pan-African Conference in Manchester.

One year before the war erupted, in the final paragraph of *Facing Mount Kenya*, Kenyatta had touched upon many of the ideas mentioned by the earlier writers:

If Africans were left in peace on their own lands, Europeans would have to offer them the benefits of white civilization in real earnest before they could obtain the African labor which they want so much. They would have to offer the African a way of life which was really superior to the one his fathers lived before him, and a share in the prosperity given them by their command of science. They would have to let the African choose what parts of European culture could be beneficially transplanted, and how they could be adapted. He would probably not choose the gas bomb or the armed police force, but he might ask for some other things of which he does not get so

14. Fred G. Burke, *Africa's Quest for Order*, p. 112.

much today. As it is, by driving him off his ancestral lands, the Europeans have robbed him of the material foundations of his culture, and reduced him to a state of servitude incompatible with human happiness. The African is conditioned, by the cultural and social institutions of centuries, to a freedom of which Europe has little conception, and it is not in his nature to accept serfdom for ever. He realizes that he must fight unceasingly for his own complete emancipation; for without this he is doomed to remain the prey of rival imperialisms, which in every successive year will drive their fangs more deeply into his vitality and strength. (p. 318)

Such, briefly, is the background, the foundation on which Africa's poets and novelists would build. They would also be influenced, of course, by the international context—by events in Ethiopia, India, China, Burma, Vietnam, North Africa, Kenya, Guinea, the Congo; by the Bandung Conference in 1955; by the presence of African nations in the United Nations; by what black men were writing in other lands, leading up to and including Richard Wright, James Baldwin, Martin Luther King, Malcolm X, and Frantz Fanon.

A significant milestone was reached in 1947 with the publication of the first issue of *Présence Africaine*. Founded by a Senegalese intellectual, Alioune Diop, and with a distinguished board of patrons which included such celebrated authors as Gide, Sartre, Camus, Richard Wright, Rivet, Emmanuel Mounier, and Leiris, this magazine provided a vehicle for the dialogue between whites and blacks; for a defense of the black man's cultural values, negritude, African personality, unity, and independence. Transcending differences of ideology, nationality, creed, and language, it ardently sought in negritude a common denominator for

English-speaker and French-speaker, revolutionary and moderate. It opened its columns to black students and black priests, to Antillean and Angolan, to Afro-Cuban and Afro-American, to Socialist, Communist, Catholic, and Moslem. By the 1950's it had founded the Société Africaine de Culture and was publishing books as well: volumes by Senghor, Cheikh Anta Diop, Birago Diop, Aimé Césaire, René Maran, Sékou Touré, Bernard Dadié; translations of W. E. B. DuBois' *Souls of Black Folk*, George Padmore's *Pan Africanism or Communism*, Melville Herskovits' *Myth of the Negro Past*. Among French-speaking Africans, one of the most influential volumes published by Présence Africaine was Cheikh Anta Diop's *Nations nègres et culture* (1955), which stressed, along with other things, the black man's contribution to Ancient Egyptian civilization. In 1956 and 1959 Présence Africaine sponsored the two Congresses of Black Writers and Artists—the first in Paris, the second in Rome. With UNESCO and the Senegalese Government, it co-sponsored the First World Festival of Negro Arts in 1966, and the International Conference of Africanists in 1967, both held in Dakar. These are but a few of its achievements, not the least of which is that it has survived.

II

Having sketched in the background, let me now preface my remarks on African fiction[15] and verse by a statistic borrowed from Charles Larson's article in *The New York Times* of April 28, 1968: "Since 1950 there have been nearly 400 volumes of poetry, prose and drama published by writers from tropical Africa" (Sec. 7, p. 2). I realize, to

15. Part of my discussion of the African novel has been published, in slightly different form, in the September 1964 issue of *Negro Digest*, in an article entitled "The African Presence."

be sure, that literature is measured not by quantity but by
quality; some of these works are mediocre, others would
reflect credit on any literature. In any event, the statistic is
astonishing when one considers the difficulties that confront the African author: the obligation to write in a foreign language, the small number of African publishers, the
low rate of literacy on their continent and, as far as the
novel is concerned, the fact that it is not a traditional
African form. There are, of course, African works in
which the note of protest is not sounded. In most, however,
it can be heard *pianissimo, forte,* or even *fortissimo.*

One of the first African novels told the story of Chaka,
the Zulu warrior.[16] The missionary-educated author,
Thomas Mofolo, of Basutoland, presented his hero as a
bloodthirsty tyrant, who owed his military successes to
witchcraft, and who even killed his relatives and his be-
loved Noliwe, sacrificing the latter to advance his own
career and increase his power. In a poem by another African Christian, Léopold Sédar Senghor, Chaka was por-
trayed in a different light; even the murder of Noliwe
found some justification. To steel himself against the cruel
trials to which the Bantu would be subjected by the "Pink
Ears," he felt obliged to stifle all emotional and family ties.

> I saw in a dream all the lands to the far corners of the
>   horizon set under the ruler, the set-square, the compass
> Forests mowed down hills leveled, valleys and rivers in
>   chains.
> I saw the lands to the four corners of the horizon under
>   the grid traced by the twofold iron ways

16. *Chaka* was first published in Basutoland in 1925; the English
translation was brought out in London in 1931; the French version was printed in Paris in 1940.

I saw the people of the South like an anthill of silence
At their work. Work is holy, but work is no longer
  gesture
Drum and voice no longer make rhythm for the gestures
  of the seasons.
Peoples of the South, in the shipyards, the ports and the
  mines and the mills
And at evening segregated in the kraals of misery.
And the peoples heap up mountains of black gold and red
  gold—and die of hunger.
I saw one morning, coming out of the mist of the dawn, a
  forest of woolly heads
Arms drooping bellies hollow, immense eyes and lips call-
  ing to an impossible god.
Could I stay deaf to such suffering, such contempt?
. . . .
I did not hate the Pink Ears. We welcomed them as
  messengers of the gods
With pleasant words and delicious drinks.
They wanted merchandise. We gave them everything:
  ivory, honey, rainbow pelts
Spices and gold, precious stones parrots and monkeys.
Shall I speak of their rusty presents, their tawdry beads?
Yes, in coming to know their guns, I became a mind
Suffering became my lot, suffering of the breast and of the
  spirit.[17]

Other historic African figures have inspired poems, dra-
mas, or novels. Significantly, these are usually people who
resisted the European invasion and were subsequently de-
picted as outlaws, despots, and/or slave-traders in accounts

17. Senghor, "Chaka," in *Selected Poems*, pp. 71–72.

written by colonialists.[18] The story of El Hadj Omar, who fought the invader and "taught Islam from the banks of the Senegal . . . to the banks of the Niger," is related by Ousmane Socé in *Contes et légendes d'Afrique Noire*. Lat Dior, a Senegalese who continued to resist for twenty years, is the hero of Amadou Cissé Dia's drama, *Les derniers jours de Lat Dior*. Aimé Césaire's recent play, *Une Saison au Congo*, eulogizes Patrice Lumumba. By the same token, on introducing a series of radio programs for the Nigerian Broadcasting Company, Dr. K. O. Dike remarked:

This attitude of hostility to the invaders of Nigeria was evident both in the Northern and Southern Regions. In fact the people who form the subjects of these essays include many nineteenth-century nationalists . . . all of whom stoutly opposed white penetration of our land; and in the process of doing so were either deposed or exiled by Britain. The point I want to make is that most of the figures in these series became famous because they preferred what nineteenth-century Europeans called "their savage independence" to being ruled under the civilizing mission of Europe. (*Eminent Nigerians of the Nineteenth Century*, pp. 6–7)

In Nyasaland (now Malawi), while en route to Ghana from his native South Africa, Alfred Hutchinson asked Dunduza Chisiza about the book the latter was carrying. "John Chilembwe," was the reply—"ever heard of him? It's about him. He is with us today." And Chisiza "rubbed the book lovingly, as if rubbing the spirit of the revolution-

---

18. Cf. Touré, *L'Expérience guinéenne et l'unité africaine*, pp. 433–434, where he observes that no history book "in our colonial schools mentions the name of the immortal chief of Labé," Alpha Yaya.

ary long since dead."[19] And there are poetic tributes to
Samory, whose military genius held off the French for
seven years; to the UPC leader and Cameroonian martyr,
Um Nyobé; to Jomo Kenyatta. In fact, these encomiums
go all the way back to Sundiata, who founded the old Mali
Empire in the thirteenth century. This type of writing
serves at least a twofold purpose: it refutes the contention
that Africa has no history, and it rehabilitates the memories
of Africa's John Browns and Nat Turners.

One attempt to classify African literature—or, more
generally, the writings of colonized people—is found in
Frantz Fanon's *The Wretched of the Earth*. The late Dr.
Fanon divided the literature of colonized peoples into three
periods: (1) an assimilationist phase; (2) a period of pre-
combat literature; and (3) the fighting phase where "instead of according the people's lethargy an honored place
in his esteem, [the author] turns himself into an awakener
of the people; hence comes a fighting literature, a revolutionary literature, and a national literature" (pp. 222–223).

With all due respect to the brilliance of Dr. Fanon's
exposition, we can still question its applicability to black
African literature, where the three periods seem to merge
into one. The first important French-African novel, René
Maran's *Batouala*, published in 1921, is as scathing and
effective a condemnation of colonialism as any African
work of fiction published since that date, and it has the
additional advantage of being written with consummate
artistry. The well-rounded picture of African life—the
literary expression of African society—will of necessity
reflect colonialism and its concomitants, but it will also
include the many other facets of the African's life: his

19. Hutchinson, *Road to Ghana*, p. 126.

culture, his problems, his essential dignity. Fanon's thesis implies that violence inspires the highest form of art. Carried to its logical conclusion, it would tend to make every black African author conform to a single pattern.

A case in point is that of the Guinean author, Camara Laye, whose excellent novel, *The African Child* (1953), was criticized by some Africans because it was not "a fighting novel of protest." One critic, writing in *Présence Africaine*, admitted that Laye is "an authentic poet," but accused him of practicing "art for art's sake," and of not measuring up to the standard set by Richard Wright in *Black Boy*. Senghor commented: "How strange of these critics to ask an artist to create not a work of art, but a polemic!" (*Liberté I,* . . . , p. 155).

Perhaps it did not occur to the reviewer that Richard Wright and Camara Laye were two distinct personalities, each writing his autobiography according to his individual talents and personal experiences, the one in Mississippi, the other in Guinea. Despite the differences in their approach, there is little doubt that *Black Boy* and *The African Child* were motivated by similar aspirations. Wright would surely have endorsed Camara Laye's statement: "Our deepest and most sensitive characteristic is our passion for independence and equality."

To justify this right to independence and equality, the black African novelist has used a wide variety of tactics: he has written subjectively, objectively, ironically, bitterly, sympathetically, in protest or defense. He has written autobiographical novels like *The African Child*, Dadié's *Climbié*, Mphahlele's *Down Second Avenue;* tales of the bush, like Maran's *Batouala* or Tutuola's *The Palm Wine Drinkard;* stories of miners in Johannesburg or railroad strikers in Senegal; tales of the teeming urban centers, like Ekwen-

si's *People of the City,* Achebe's *No Longer at Ease,* or
Mongo Beti's *Ville cruelle;* political novels, such as Abrahams' *A Wreath for Udomo* and Achebe's *A Man of the
People;* legends and historical novels, like Mofolo's *Chaka;*
tales of transplanted Africans in Paris, London, or New
York. This multiple approach has made his works more
readable, has carried his message to different types of readers, has emphasized the human qualities of his people. But
he has not pulled his punches.

III

Three or four key words will facilitate our survey of this
fiction and poetry. The first of these is *civilization.* "To
civilize the savages"—such was the pretext used by the
colonizer to justify his invasion of the so-called Dark Continent. As early as 1921, in the preface of *Batouala,* René
Maran attacked it: "Civilization, civilization, pride of Europeans and their slaughter-house of innocents, Rabindran-
ath Tagore, the Hindu poet, once, in Tokyo, told what you
are! You build your kingdom on corpses. Whatever you
wish, whatever you do, is steeped in lies. . . . You are not a
torch, but a fire. Whatever you touch, you devour." African poets agreed; witness this from Senghor's first volume
of verse, *Chants d'ombre:* "They cut down the forests of
Africa to save Civilization, for there was a shortage of
human raw-material." And this from a Senegalese student
in 1952:

> But here come the "Civilizers"
> with cannon and Bible aimed
> at the African's heart.[20]

20. Amadou Moustapha Wade, in *Les Etudiants noirs parlent,*
p. 202.

Later a Cameroonian poet would write a poem entitled
"Civilisation" (translated here from the French):

> They found me in the healthy shade
> of my bamboo hut
> they found me
> dressed in *obom* and animal skins
> with my palavers
> and my torrential laughter
> with my tom toms
>> my gris-gris
>> and my gods
>
> What a pity! How primitive he is!
> Let's civilize him.
> Then they showered my head
> with their wordy books
> then they bedecked my body
> with their own gris-gris
> then they inoculated me
> in my blood
> my bright transparent blood
> with avarice
> and alcoholism
> and prostitution
> and incest
> and fratricidal politics
>
> Hurrah!
> Behold me now, a civilized man![21]

All over black Africa, "an Africa disillusioned by what
Western civilization had done to her,"[22] the story was the

21. Philombe, in *Neuf Poètes camerounais*, p. 86.
22. Hutchinson, *Road to Ghana*, p. 125.

same. In Johannesburg, Peter Abrahams saw European civilization through the eyes of black miners "huddled together like cattle in a cattle truck," en route to the mines:

As a child I had often watched them tumble out of the
railway trucks. As a child I had always laughed when the
induna cursed them for the wild and stupidly frightened animals they were. I had seen the fear and the strangeness in their
eyes. I had laughed when the shrill blast of the engine sent
them running like frightened rabbits. It had amused me greatly
to watch a column of them scurrying, panic-stricken, through
the heavy traffic of the Johannesburg streets. It had been such
fun when some White motorist, bent on having fun at the
expense of the "raw kaffirs," crawled up to the column and
then suddenly let out a loud blast on his horn. And what fun,
what cause for laughter, when a fear-crazed Black ran into a
lamp-post and knocked himself silly! Or when they scattered
in all directions, causing traffic hold-ups! Or when they fell
over themselves trying to get out of the way of the terrifying
traffic! And the horns would blare. And the Whites in their
cars would be at a circus watching apes perform.

I went back to see if these things still happened. They did.
My childhood laughter came back to mock me. But the heirs
and guardians of some strange thing called "European civilization" still laughed and found it amusing. (*Return to Goli*, p.
100)

Later Nona Jabavu tells us, in *The Ochre People*,
"apartheid was becoming like a granite wall to defend
white civilization, because Dr. Verwoerd was at the time
urging his followers to make it so" (p. 154). Another South
African, a fugitive from the infamous Treason Trial, describes Christianity in Africa as "a farce. In South Africa

everything is done in the name of Christian civilization. It's synonymous with white civilization—white supremacy. I don't think we need those bonds."[23] In Nyasaland the exile was told: "The *Mzungus* (whites) are full of rubbish. . . . Dawn had come to Nyasaland. The white ruler must go. To hell with his partnerships and federations! Independence for Nyasaland now!"[24]

In Kenya, driven to revolt by segregation, exploitation, and the theft of their lands, Kikuyu suspected of taking the Mau Mau oath were tortured in concentration camps:

"Once bottlenecks were hammered into people's backsides, and the men whimpered like caged animals. . . . When I was young, I saw the white man, I did not know who he was or where he came from. Now I know that a Mzungu is not a man —always remember that—he is a devil—devil." He paused again to gain breath, and resumed his subdued voice, "I saw a man whose manhood was broken with pincers. He came out of the screening office and fell down and he cried: to know I will never touch my wife again, oh God, can I ever look at her in the eyes after this?" (Ngugi, *A Grain of Wheat*, p. 209)

That, too, was an aspect of Western civilization as reported by the African writer. Small wonder that a Nigerian novelist asked the rhetorical question: "What is civilization but silver-gilt savagery?"[25]

In one of Maran's stories, Bokorro, the python, asked Moumeu, the crocodile: "What's a white man?" "A white man is a man who is not black," the omniscient Moumeu replied, hastening to add: "but the white man knows how to handle the lightning-stick." The use and abuse of that lightning-stick made an indelible impact on the African

23. Hutchinson, *Road to Ghana*, p. 186.
24. Hutchinson, *Road to Ghana*, p. 104.
25. Nzekwu, *Wand of Noble Wood*, p. 58.

novel; violence became the main ingredient of the white man's civilization. As Kenya's Tom Mboya has said:

Too many journalists and sensational writers . . . have interpreted Africa as a continent of violence and bloodshed. Being patient and unusually good-humored people, we are amused that this should be the view of white men who have started two world wars and burned up thousands of civilians with atomic bombs, and even now crouch in terror lest their opponents in East or West may loose their huge nuclear armories in their direction. Is this what they call freedom?" (*Freedom and After*, p. 262)

Similar examples of inconsistency and injustice are singled out by the novelists. One grievance frequently mentioned is the wage differential, the colonizer's reluctance to give equal pay for equal work. "It isn't the labor but the color that they pay," a Malian complains in Seydou Badian's *Sous l'orage*. "A skilled miner is one who has a white face," reports Peter Abrahams, in *Return to Goli*. "When a white miner does a drilling job, it becomes a skilled job. When a black miner does it, it is unskilled" (p. 211). Even in the civil service (in colonial Kenya), says Abrahams, "an African or Asian doing the same job as a European would get only three-fifths of the European's pay, while a European woman would get four-fifths" (p. 211). In Senegal a railway worker urges his comrades to strike:

"We are the ones who do the work," he roared, "and it's the same work the whites do. So, what right have they to earn more? Because they're white? And when they are sick, why are they taken care of; why do we and our families merely have the right to die? Because we are black? In what respect is a white child better than a black child? In what respect is a

white worker better than a black worker? We are told that we
have equal rights, but that's a lie, nothing but a lie! The
machine that we run, the machine tells the truth: it recognizes
neither white nor black. What good is it to look at our pay
slips and say we don't make enough? If we want to live
decently, we've got to fight." (Ousmane, *Les Bouts de bois de
Dieu*, p. 24)

In short, our authors found that civilization meant education and exploitation, hospitals and haughtiness, Christianity and segregated churches, money and misery, knowledge
but not wisdom, progress but not partnership. The African
wanted the progress, but he also wanted to retain the more
valid, human aspects of his own culture. The more he saw
of the European, at home or abroad, the more convinced he
became that his own way of life possessed qualities worthy
of being preserved. "There are two worlds," says a character in a Cameroonian novel; "ours is a world of respect and
mystery and magic. Their world brings everything into the
daylight, even the things that weren't meant to be."[26] In one
of Birago Diop's magnificent *Contes d'Amadou Koumba*,
the author defends initiation rites that teach a boy to resist
pain. He even defends the use of masks and statuettes,
finding them at least as useful as the masks worn by Europeans at the Mardi Gras in Nice. "It is true, however, that
the whites wore masks just for fun and not to teach children the rudiments of ancestral wisdom" (p. 184).

In the words of Ezekiel Mphahlele, still another South
African exile from the Treason Trial:

I admire the white man's achievements, his mind that plans tall
buildings, powerful machinery. I used to want to justify my-

---

26. Oyono, *Une Vie de boy*, p. 123.

self and my own kind to the white man. I later discovered that it wasn't worth it. It was to myself and to my kind I needed to justify myself. I think now the white man has no right to tell me how to order my life as a social being. . . . He may teach me how to make a shirt or to read and write, but my forebears and I could teach him a thing or two if only he would listen and allow himself time to feel. Africa is no more for the white man who comes here to teach and to control her human and material forces and not to learn. (*Down Second Avenue*, p. 218)

Our novelists reject, among other things, the European's greed—"*a white man has never wanted anything except to make money*"; his arrogance—"*What do they bring you? Nothing. What do they leave you? Nothing but scorn for your own people, for those who gave you life*"; his hypocrisy—"*They only seek to fool you*"; his injustice—"*Even in those days I knew that all colonial systems have one thing in common: the cudgel.*" The italicized rejoinders come from two novels by Mongo Beti, of Cameroon: *Ville cruelle* and *Mission terminée*. Occasionally there are humane Europeans in this fiction—the old French lady in Camara Laye's *Dramouss* who helps African students in Paris; Kocoumbo's benefactor in Aké Loba's *Kocoumbo, l'étudiant noir;* Climbié's friend; the wife in Sembène Ousmane's *O Pays mon beau peuple*, etc.—but these are the exceptions to prove the rule enunciated by the aged African in Jabavu's *The Ochre People:* "God sent them [the whites] as a plague to try us."

Many characters in these novels are imprisoned, often without real justification. The hero of *Une Vie de boy* is incarcerated because he knows that the lady for whom he works is having an affair with the prison warden. (Her husband also is aware of the liaison but can forgive adultery more readily than he can forget that his African servant knows about the wife's infidelity.) Down Mphahlele's Second Avenue in Pretoria, Africans are imprisoned for brewing and selling beer. Even Méka, the law-abiding hero of Ferdinand Oyono's *Le vieux nègre et la médaille,* spends a night in jail because he drank a bit too much and fell asleep a few hours after the French had decorated him as a model African. In view of the frequency with which the prison appears in this fiction, one would be tempted to consider it the symbol of colonialist civilization. Indeed, as one Senegalese author noted in 1952, "One could easily show that there are, for example, more prisons than dispensaries because the police system penetrates even the smallest communities, while this is not true of the health services."[27] Novelist James Ngugi, in *A Grain of Wheat,* calls the Police Station "a symbol of that might which dominated Kenya to the door of every hut. Destroy that, and the whiteman is gone" (p. 111).

Often our authors depict the weaknesses of Western ideas and institutions with a fine sense of irony. In Chinua Achebe's *Things Fall Apart* (1958), the District Commissioner, who has wrought havoc in a Nigerian community, muses over the title of the book he is planning: "The Pacification of the Primitive Tribes of the Lower Niger." In the same novel, three converts join the brand new European church after "it became known that the white man's fetish had unbelievable power. It was said that he wore glasses so that he could see and talk to evil spirits" (p. 134). Nor was the youngster in Oyono's *Une Vie de boy* attracted to the missionary by any zeal for spiritual renewal:

27. Abdoulaye Wade, "Afrique Noire et Union Française," in *Les Etudiants noirs parlent,* p. 130.

"I just wanted to get close to the white man . . . who dressed in woman's clothes and gave little black boys lumps of sugar" (p. 18). Moreover, the missionary's pronunciation of the local African language which transformed respectable words into obscenities also assured his success. Despairing because so many converts became backsliders, the missionary in Mongo Beti's *Le pauvre Christ de Bomba* is told:

The first of us who ran to religion, to your religion, came as if to a revelation; that's it, a revelation, a school where they would acquire the revelation of your secret, the secret of your strength, the power of your airplanes, your railroads, and what-not. Instead, you began to talk to them about God, the soul, eternal life, etc. Do you imagine that they didn't know about all that already, long before your arrival? Indeed, they had a feeling that you were holding something from them. Later they perceived that with money they could get lots of things, phonographs, for example, automobiles, and perhaps airplanes someday. (p. 56)

This willingness to share the white man's secrets and technical accomplishments by no means indicates docile acceptance of his way of life, his religion, or even his education. The hero's aunt in Kane's *L'Aventure ambiguë* detests the foreigner's school but insists that her nephew attend it. "Years ago," she explains, "our grandfathers and the elite of the country were defeated. Why? How? Only the newcomers know. We must ask them; we must go learn from them the art of conquering without being in the right" (p. 52). The chief protagonist of a Cameroonian novel sets himself up in business as a guide for tourists:

. . . enabling them to photograph or film pygmies or monkeys swaying on a branch, a boa constrictor swollen up as he painfully digests his prey, a hippopotamus scampering down a riverbank, or a married couple shaking their heads to the rhythm of a balafon. These were so many scenes that the tourists dubbed *"Formidable!" "Extraordinaire!" "Sensationnel!"* My compatriots improvised in this way a ritual which the latter-day explorers filmed while smiling at the thought that at the next film festival they would . . . win first prize and become consecrated as Africanists. (Oyono, *Chemin d'Europe*, p. 116)

In a more recent novel from Cameroon, the villagers dig holes in the road during rainy season and cover them with mud. Then the European motorist is compelled to pay them for getting his car out of the rut. This brings a certain amount of prosperity to the community. "Today," says the hero, "when I hear people assert that a road is one of the signs of progress, I wonder if they realize how right they are."[28]

The irony continues as an author from the Ivory Coast, unjustly imprisoned a few years before, observes while visiting the French capital: "Paris would be the last capital to put chains on other men."[29] A Gambian student traveling by train in England comments: "My fellow passengers in the compartment were behaving as though they had not seen me, and I supposed that this must be the traditional way of welcoming a stranger in Britain."[30] Surprised to discover that the British bathe less frequently at home than they do when in West Africa, the same student generalizes: "Throughout history conquered peoples have taught their conquerors good habits." Batouala's father ends a discussion

28. Bebey, *Le Fils d'Agatha Moudio*, p. 147.
29. Dadié, *Un Nègre à Paris*, p. 192.
30. Conton, *The African*, p. 56.

of the European's shortcomings by recommending a Rabe-
laisian solution: "We would do better to grumble less about
the whites and to drink more. You know as well as I that,
except for the bed, Pernod is the only important invention
of the European."[31]

Perhaps the outstanding example of African irony is
found in Camara Laye's second novel, *Le Regard du roi*
(translated as *The Radiance of the King*). A European,
who has come to Africa to seek his fortune, starts out by
gambling away his money and being ejected from his hotel.
With nothing to recommend him but his whiteness, he
hopes none the less to obtain a position from the King.
Unable to get the audience, he is later used as a stud,
producing mulatto babies for an aging local chief. At the
end of the story he is finally admitted to the royal presence,
but only after he has completely reversed the values of
European civilization.

In much the same manner the poets also use ridicule in
their critique of a sick society. In Wole Soyinka's "Telephone Conversation," the Nigerian calls up a prospective
landlady to inquire about lodging. To save himself a trip
across London only to risk a rebuff because of his color, he
tells her that he is African, fearful all the while lest she hang
up (hence the reference to Button A, Button B, another
refinement of Western technology). I quote the end of the
poem:

Silence. Silenced transmission of
Pressurized good breeding. Voice, when it came,
Lipstick-coated, long gold rolled
Cigarette-holder pipped. Caught I was, foully.
HOW DARK? I had not misheard. ARE YOU LIGHT

31. Maran, *Batouala*, p. 100.

OR VERY DARK? Button B. Button A. Stench of rancid
  breath of public hide-and-speak.
. . . .
Considerate she was, varying the emphasis—
ARE YOU DARK OR VERY LIGHT? Revelation
  came.
You mean—like plain or milk chocolate?
Her assent was clinical, crushing in its light
Impersonality. Rapidly, wave-length adjusted,
I chose. "West African sepia"—and as afterthought,
"Down in my passport." Silence for spectroscopic
Flight of fancy, till truthfulness changed her accent
Hard on the mouthpiece. "WHAT'S THAT?" Conced-
  ing
"DON'T KNOW WHAT THAT IS." "Like brunette."
"THAT'S DARK, ISN'T IT?" "Not altogether.
Facially, I am brunette, but madam, you should see
The rest of me. Palm of my hand, soles of my feet
Are a peroxide blonde. Friction caused—
Foolishly, madam—by sitting down, has turned
My bottom raven black. . . . One moment, madam!" . . .
  sensing
Her receiver rearing on the thunderclap
About my ears—"Madam," I pleaded, "wouldn't you
  rather
See for yourself?"[32]

Another Nigerian, Gabriel Okara, in "Once upon a
time," describes another result of Western civilization:

> Once upon a time, son
>
> they used to laugh with their hearts

32. In Moore and Beier, *Modern Poetry from Africa*, pp. 111–
112.

and laugh with their eyes;
but now they only laugh with their teeth,
while their ice-block-cold eyes
search behind my shadow.

There was a time indeed
they used to shake hands with their hearts;
but that's gone, son.
Now they shake hands without hearts
while their left hands search
my empty pockets.

"Feel at home," "Come again,"
they say, and when I come
again and feel
at home, once, twice,
there will be no thrice—
for then I find doors shut on me.

So I have learned many things, son,
I have learned to wear many faces
like dresses—homeface,
officeface, streetface, hostface, cock-
tailface, with all their conforming smiles
like a fixed portrait smile

And I have learned too
to laugh with only my teeth
and shake hands without my heart.
I have also learned to say, "Goodbye,"
when I mean "Goodriddance":
to say "Glad to meet you,"
without being glad; and to say "It's been
nice talking to you," after being bored.

But believe me, son
I want to be what I used to be

when I was like you. I want
to unlearn all these muting things.
Most of all, I want to relearn
how to laugh, for my laugh in the mirror
shows only my teeth like a snake's bare fangs!

So show me, son
how to laugh; show me how
I used to laugh and smile
Once upon a time when I was like you.[33]

Nor do we Americans escape the barbs of the African's
irony. Often the target is our most vulnerable point: race
relations. Ousmane Socé, in *Mirages de Paris*, points out
that despite lynchings and various laws against miscegena-
tion, there are more mulattoes in the United States than in
any other country (p. 201). Apropos of American justice,
the Nigerian poet and playwright J. P. Clark wonders
"whether those two in happy concert, the American government and people, included the Negro as well" (*America, Their America*, p. 170). Another Nigerian, Chinua
Achebe, relates the following incident in his most recent
novel, *A Man of the People:* An American Negro, seated at
a table in a Lagos hotel, is approached by a white American:

"May I join you, sir?"
"Sure," replied the other.
"What do you think of the Peace Corps?"

33. In Hughes, *Poems from Black Africa*, p. 87. Dadié, also,
regrets that many urban Africans have replaced their "cordial,
thunderous, inimitable, warm, generous African laughter" by an
"oblique, fixed, sad, sapless smile . . . coming from the lips, not
from the heart which 'has to become civilized'" (*Climbié*, pp.
127–128).

"I've nothing against it. One of my daughters is in it."
"You American?"
"Sure. I came over . . ."

The Nigerian author adds the punch line: "I could see the other man promptly excusing himself and searching other tables for *authentic* Africans" (p. 57).

Harlem, to the Ivory Coast poet and novelist, Bernard Dadié, is "the camp of the shipwrecked, of orphans mistreated by a stepmother, the camp of men to be integrated but for the time being wrapped up in jazz as in an iron corset. Each night Harlem blows its trumpet of Jericho at the feet of Wall Street. Harlem, funeral home of America where Negro tears are taken for cries of joy" (*Patron de New-York*, p. 140). Similarly, a Senegalese poet, Assane Diallo, writes in a poem called "Blues":

> Alabama Negro
> whose meat
> tastes sweet
> to police dogs
>
> Harlem Negro
> whose heartsore
> is folklore
> to blasé customers[34]

Bernard Dadié paints an amusing picture of the Boston Tea Party, in *Patron de New-York*, noting incidentally that the first to die for American liberty was a black man "with a provocative name: Crispus Attucks."

Let London, Southampton, Liverpool be burned, that doesn't matter, they can be rebuilt. But burning shipments of tea was

---

34. In *Nouvelle Somme de poésie du monde noir*, p. 134.

going too far. The national beverage! That was not only the
ultimate in scorn but also the most brazen provocation. And
there are acts that national honor cannot tolerate. . . . The
British lion was wounded in its most sensitive spot. The national beverage! Condemning thousands of citizens to die of
thirst! Such an affront could be washed away only in blood.
. . . This war would last for seven years, as long, embarrassing,
and exhausting as a European war. . . . The whites noted with
astonishment that the Negro's blood was red. . . . Each was
waging his war: the Negro for his freedom, the white to
protect his interests which included the black man. (pp.
29–31)

Seven pages later Dadié suggests that one of the fifty stars
in the American flag should be black, as a permanent reminder "that there are American Negroes on this continent
and that they too have rights as citizens" (p. 38).

   Numerous other charges, not necessarily connected with
racism, are brought against the United States. On several
occasions in his *Patron de New-York*, Dadié accuses this
country of trying to rule the world, of wanting "to be the
conductor of a universal symphony" (p. 133).[35] Aimé Césaire, in *Discours sur le colonialisme*, is more explicit and
much more embittered: "The hour of the barbarian has

   35. Cf. also Césaire's *Une Saison au Congo*, p. 55, where the
Great Western Ambassador rattles the saber: "I know well that as
a nation we have a bad reputation. We are accused of being quick
on the draw, but when . . . nations are boiling over, can one
follow a rocking-chair policy? When nations do not conduct themselves decently, someone has to bring them back to decency.
Providence has entrusted that task to us. Thank you, Lord. Well,
let it be known, we are not only the world's policemen, we are
also the world's firemen. Firemen prepared to circumscribe everywhere any fire lighted by communist pyromania."

arrived. The modern barbarian. The American hour. Violence, excessiveness, waste, mercantilism, bluff, gregariousness, stupidity, vulgarity, disorder" (pp. 68–69). A wealthy Nigerian offering 50,000 pounds for "a seat in the House at the next elections" and "the Minister of Consolation out of the way," is told that he talks "like an American. . . . Americans see red in everything. And it's the reds who see revolution in everything."[36] Even Senghor, the apostle of conciliation, sometimes upbraids the Americans for their materialism, their worship of the machine, their neglect of the human. Here are a few lines from his famous poem "New York":

> But two weeks on the bare sidewalks of Manhattan
> —At the end of the third week the fever seizes you with
>   the pounce of a leopard
> Two weeks without rivers or fields, all the birds of the air
> Falling sudden and dead on the high ashes of flat rooftops.
> No smile of a child blooms, his hand refreshed in my
>   hand,
> No mother's breast, but only nylon legs. Legs and breasts
>   that have no sweat or smell.
> No tender words for there are no lips, only artificial
>   hearts paid for in hard cash
> And no book where wisdom may be read. . . .
> . . . .
> New York! I say to you: New York let black blood flow
>   into your blood
> That it may rub the rust from your steel joints, like an oil
>   of life,

36. Ekwensi, *Beautiful Feathers,* p. 86.

That it may give to your bridges the bend of buttocks and
the suppleness of creepers.[37]

African disapproval of United States policy, foreign and
domestic, lessened somewhat under the impact of a John F.
Kennedy, who captured the imagination and the hearts of
blacks as no other American president had ever done. His
assassination, however, in the opinion of all the Africans
with whom I have discussed it, was somehow related to his
espousal of civil rights. Take for example these lines from
Lamine Diakhaté's "Sur le tombeau de John Kennedy":

Then you spoke the message forgotten
since LINCOLN
Surprised in their tranquillity, the caciques
shook their mane heavy with the weight of laziness
They could not understand
They did not recognize you
They accused you of not speaking their language
Your message reverberated to the four corners of the
    Union
Respectable folk turned their back on you
Your voice seemed to them more violent
than any ever heard by an American
Their tranquillity disturbed, the caciques vowed to get
    you.[38]

Continued private American investment in South Africa,
Vietnam, our airlift in the Congo, our partnership in

37. I have quoted from the translation of Gerald Moore and
Ulli Beier, *Modern Poetry from Africa*, pp. 51–53.
38. From Diakhaté's *Temps de mémoire*, p. 57; translation
my own. See also in the same volume a poem on the 1963 Freedom
March, another "De Selma à Montgomery," and a third on George
Wallace, entitled "Démence."

NATO with Portugal, our reduced foreign aid and, more recently, the murders of Martin Luther King and another Kennedy have done little to improve our image on the African continent.[39]

As these poets and novelists review the crimes committed by the so-called civilization, they detect unmistakable portents of decadence and death. "Civilization!" Lamine Niang exclaims in *Négristique*, "I hear muted the bell tolling your death." Dadié sees America "hanging on to the world in order not to sink under its gold and its machines, to avoid being smothered under the weight of its tons of dollars" (*Patron de New-York*, p. 292). And there is Césaire's famous verbal explosion in *Cahier d'un retour au pays natal*.[40]

> Listen to the white world
> horribly exhausted by its immense effort

39. The results of two surveys of French-speaking African student opinion should be reported in this connection. The first, undertaken by a young Senegalese sociologist in 1961, questioned 294 African students in France. Asked to name the country they admired most, 25 per cent selected the Soviet Union; 20 per cent, Communist China; 12.4 per cent, Israel; 12 per cent, Cuba; 8 per cent, France; 6 per cent, Switzerland; 3.3 per cent, the U.S.A. (see J. P. N'Diaye, *Enquête sur les étudiants noirs en France*, Paris: Éditions Réalités Africaines, 1962, p. 244). The second poll, conducted at the University of Dakar in 1962 by a professor of sociology, obtained the following response to a similar question: France was the model nation for 22 per cent; Switzerland, 15 per cent; U.S.S.R., 14 per cent; Israel, 12 per cent; Cuba, 6 per cent; Communist China, 5 per cent; India, 3 per cent; U.S.A., 3 per cent (see Pierre Fougeyrollas, *Modernisation des hommes*, Paris: Flammarion, 1967, pp. 146–148). Both polls were taken shortly after the murder of Patrice Lumumba, which intensified anti-Western feeling throughout much of Africa.

40. Quoted from the Brentano edition (1947), n.p.

its rebellious joints cracking under the hard stars
. . . .
Pity for our omniscient naive conquerors!
Hurrah for those who never invented anything
for those who never explored anything
for those who never conquered anything!

By the same token, Senghor, laden down with honors
from the French university, warns his compatriots: "We
must assimilate, not be assimilated." In his "Prayer for
Peace," he asks God to forgive white Europe:

Lord, forgive them who turned the Askia into *maquisards,*
my princes into sergeant-majors
My household servants into 'boys', my peasants into wage-
earners, my people into a working class.
For Thou must forgive those who have hunted my chil-
dren like wild elephants,
And broken them in with whips, have made them the
black hands of those whose hands were white.
For Thou must forget those who exported ten millions
of my sons in the leperhouses of their ships
Who killed two hundred millions of them
And have made for me a solitary old age in the forest of
my nights and the savannah of my days.
Lord, the glasses of my eyes grow dim
And lo, the serpent of hatred raises its head in my heart,
that serpent that I believed was dead.[41]

To be sure, later in this moving poem, which Senghor
dedicates to his former classmate Georges Pompidou and
Mme Pompidou, he again crushes the serpent of hatred
while looking forward to a new kind of civilization in

41. *Selected Poems,* p. 49. This poem was written in 1945.

which all races and cultures will join on a basis of peace, equality, and justice. Senghor often defines this as "the Civilization of the Universal," preferring this term to that of "Universal Civilization" which has historic overtones of white monopoly. Similarly, another member of the Présence Africaine group, poet Jacques Rabemananjara of Madagascar, says: "What you call universal is for us a completely truncated universal, since we were absent from it. We were not included in that 'universal' and I cannot see how that idea can be defined as 'universal' while a great portion of humanity did not figure in it!"[42]

Perhaps the angriest and certainly one of the most gifted of African poets was David Diop, of Senegal, who died in an airplane crash at the age of thirty-three. In tones reminiscent of a young Langston Hughes, one of his early poems described "the time of martyrdom":

The white man killed my father
My father was proud
The white man raped my mother
My mother was beautiful
The white man bent my brother under the highway sun
My brother was strong
The white man turned toward me
His hands red with black blood
And in the voice of a Master:
"Hey boy! bring me a whiskey, a napkin, and some
    water!"[43]

Note the first five lines of his poem "The Vultures":

42. *Comprendre*, No. 21–22, p. 227.
43. *Coups de Pilon*, p. 34. This poem was originally published in 1948.

In those days
When civilization kicked us in the face
When holy water slapped our cringing brows
The vultures built in the shadow of their talons
The bloodstained monument of tutelage[44]

IV

So much for the African's indictment of "civilization."
Our second key word is *identity*.[45] Unable to identify with
the world as presently constituted, the African leader, by
and large, has refused to become aligned with either side in
the Cold War. "Positive neutralism," Nkrumah has called
it. "In order to be truly influential the New Africans feel
that they must remain unaligned to either of the two big-
gest power blocs. They must achieve their own identity
and self respect." So writes South African exile, Lewis
Nkosi,[46] while Boubou Hama, President of Niger's National Assembly and a distinguished historian, likens the
Cold War to a rope-pull with the United States and Soviet
Union tugging away, each likely to fall down the deep
precipice just behind them.[47] Africa's hope, in the view of
these writers, lies in a neutrality that may offer a third
choice (and a last chance) to the world.

Geographically, various authors remind us, Africa re-
sembles a question mark. It must answer for itself, develop

44. In Moore and Beier, *Modern Poetry from Africa*, p. 59.
45. Cf. two recent books on the subject: William H. Lewis,
French-speaking Africa: A Search for Identity (New York:
Walker, 1965); Victor Ferkis, *Africa's Search for Identity* (New
York: Braziller, 1965).
46. See "Black Power or Souls of Black Writers," in Gordimer
and Abrahams, *South African Writing Today*.
47. Hama, *Enquête sur les fondements et la genèse de l'unité
africaine*, p. 516.

its own resourcefulness and its own personality. As Tom Mboya told the delegates to the First All-African Peoples' Conference in December 1958, Africa must no longer be considered an appendage to Europe or any other continent. This, basically, is what Senghor means by his warning to "assimilate, not be assimilated." This, indeed, is why Nkrumah urged his fellow Africans: "Seek ye first the political kingdom." Why else did Sékou Touré tell de Gaulle in 1958: "We prefer poverty in freedom to riches in slavery"? A bit later in the same speech, the Guinean leader said:

Speaking of Franco-African relations, some people argue exclusively on economic and social grounds, and conclude inevitably, because of the great backwardness of underdeveloped African nations, by excusing France's colonial action. These men forget that above the economic and the social, there is a more important value that orients and determines most often the action of Africans: this superior value lies essentially in the conscience that Africans bring to the political struggle, straining to safeguard their dignity and originality and to free their personality completely. (*L'Expérience guinéenne*, p. 77)

Still seeking his own identity as an African, he wondered, in another speech later that month, why "Whenever we take a plane or a boat, we have to declare ourselves each time: M. Sékou Touré, nationality: French!" (p. 97). So much is involved here: a sense of dignity, a knowledge of and respect for one's past, determination that Africa, through independence, solidarity, and intelligent, persistent effort, shall know a better future.

This search for identity could be illustrated by many examples from contemporary African literature. It is the quest so beautifully described by Davidson Nicol as he

returns home to Sierra Leone with his doctorate from
London; I quote part of "The Continent That Lies within
Us":

> . . . You are not a country,
> Africa, you are a concept, which we all
> Fashion in our minds, each to each, to
> Hide our separate years, to dream our separate dreams.
> Only those within you who know their circumscribed
> Plot, and till it well with steady plow
> Can from that harvest then look up
> To the vast blue inside of the enamelled bowl of sky,
> Which covers you and say, "This is my Africa," meaning
> "I am content and I am happy. I am fulfilled, within,
> Without and roundabout. I have gained the little
> Longings of my hands, my heart, my skin, and the soul
> That follows in my shadow."
> I know now that is what you are, Africa,
> Happiness, contentment and fulfillment,
> And a small bird singing on a mango tree.[48]

Our second illustration of the search is a poem by a
Liberian poet, Roland Tombekai Dempster:

Africa's Plea

> I am not you—
> but you will not
> give me a chance
> will not let me be *me*.
>
> "If I were you"—
> but you know
> I am not you

48. Entitled "The Meaning of Africa," in Hughes, *Poems from Black Africa*, pp. 42–43.

yet you will not
let me be *me*.

You meddle, interfere
in my affairs
as if they were yours
and you were me.

You are unfair, unwise
foolish to think
that I can be you
talk, act
and think like you.

God made me *me*.
He made you *you*.
For God's sake
Let me be *me*.[49]

What Mr. Dempster is pleading for here in general terms
is spelled out in greater detail by other African authors; for
example, by Wole Soyinka, Nigeria's leading dramatist,
who ridicules compatriots still afflicted by an inferiority
complex and slavishly imitating the white man. In *The
Lion and the Jewel* (pp. 36–37), one such character pre-
dicts:

Within a year or two, I swear,
This town shall see a transformation
Bride-price will be a thing forgotten
And wives shall take their place by men.
A motor road will pass this spot
And bring the city ways to us.

. . . .

49. In Hughes, *Poems from Black Africa*, p. 81.

> The ruler shall ride cars, not horses
> Or a bicycle at the very least.
> We'll burn the forest, cut the trees
> Then plant a modern park for lovers
> We'll print newspapers every day
> With pictures of seductive girls.
> The world will judge our progress by
> The girls that win beauty contests
> . . . .
> Where is our school of Ballroom dancing?
> Who here can throw a cocktail party?
> We must be modern with the rest
> Or live forgotten by the world
> We must reject the palm wine habit
> And take to tea, with milk and sugar.

By the same token, in a poem by a Malian, a wife objects because her husband has changed his African name to Victor-Emile-Louis-Henri-Joseph, has stopped eating homegrown African food, ceased wearing African clothes, and gone into debt. She concludes:

> Before, I was underdeveloped
> Now, thanks to you, I've become undernourished[50]

Others resent the ban on speaking African languages in the schools. This sometimes leads to amusing results, as in an incident reported by Oyono in *Une Vie de boy:* on a special occasion, in the presence of their parents and an official French delegation, school children sang "La Marseillaise." The parents thought their offspring were singing in French, while the French were certain that the young-

50. "A mon mari," by Ouologuem Yambo, in *Nouvelle Somme de poésie du monde noir*, p. 95.

sters were singing in the local African tongue. The author
assures his readers that it was neither French nor African.

In Niamey last summer we were surprised to find a poem
on the subject in the July 15, 1968, issue of the weekly *Le
Niger*. Roughly translated, it reads as follows:

Lapsus

You're free, they told me
but still they persecute me
I liberate you, they told me
but why do they pursue me?
They killed my father—for their roads
They deprived my mother of love—for their sons
They kidnaped my sister—for their pleasure
They humiliated my wife—for her fidelity
Then they told me, you're free
But still they persecute me.
I was pure as the river.
I understood nature
The stars spoke to me
The language of the wind was mine
The lightning flash to me a sign
But they taught me their science
And I doubted. . . .
. . . .
Then they told me, you're free
When will I be me?

—Bania Mahamadou Say

The search for identity, which Ferkis calls "the basic
dynamic of African politics," is proceeding against a back-
drop of violence in Nigeria, the Portuguese colonies, and
potential revolt in Rhodesia and South Africa—much of

which, especially the South African situation—is reflected in the literature. Nkosi warns:

The first thing to learn . . . is that a New African is abroad, and that, the world being what it is, failure to recognize him is going to bring all of us to perilous times. This is no idle talk. Dr. Verwoerd is at this moment sitting on a powder keg. Beneath this powder keg is a vast mineral wealth which is urgently needed to set Africa on her way to achieving economic self-reliance; and if there should be an explosion in Southern Africa the rest of the continent would never be the same again. (*South African Writing Today*, p. 195)

The immediate challenge is, of course, the situation in Nigeria, a conflict pitting one group of Black Africans against another group of Black Africans, despite the proverb quoted by Chinua Achebe in *No Longer at Ease*, to the effect that "anger against a brother is felt in the flesh, not in the bone" (p. 5). This obstacle in the path of African unity also threatens the search for identity, for the identification must eventually be made in terms of Africa, or at least according to national entities, rather than in terms of Hausa, Ibo, Yoruba, Fulani, Wolof, Serer, Diola, Ashanti, Ewe, Kikuyu, or Luo. One of the arguments advanced against negritude was that it failed to encompass Arabs and Berbers. Senghor tried to meet this objection by enlarging the term to "Africanité" on his official visit to Cairo in February 1967 and by composing as the last line of Senegal's national anthem: "The Bantu is a brother, and the Arab, and the white man." Nkrumah avoided the difficulty by selecting "African personality" as the rallying cry.

In a volume published while he was Ghana's representative at the United Nations, Ambassador Quaison-Sackey

noted some of the differences between negritude and the
African personality:

Although Negritude stresses a common conditioning, a common cultural background, and seeks to reconcile Negro culture with Western culture, the African Personality, by confin-
ing itself to the African continent, accomplishes all that Negritude seeks and a good deal more. For the African Personality
seeks first to find itself before it attempts to seek reconciliation,
and it takes action, creative action, in trying to realize the
dreams of Negritude, with which, of course, it has nothing but
sympathy and understanding, to which it is closely related. Yet
the proponents of Negritude are, by and large, "exiles"—
which is to say that they have not lived in the home of their
ancestors; the proponents of the African Personality are conscious of their ancient roots, and from this sense of tradition
they gain their strength, in action, in the struggle toward
individual emancipation and national realization. (*Africa Unbound*, p. 49)

Negritude is taken less seriously by some of the other
English-speaking African authors. Who has not heard
Wole Soyinka's famous quip about a tiger not proclaiming
his tigritude (which Senghor has ascribed to "an inferiority
complex inoculated by the colonizer")? A character in
Soyinka's novel, *The Interpreters*, treats it flippantly on
two occasions: "Those whiskies burnt out all my negritude" (p. 34), and "For four days the sun had remained
hidden. 'I could do with some negritude,' Sagoe moaned,
'anything to keep me warm'" (p. 107). Viewing the concept from the South African perspective, Ezekiel Mphahlele observes, in *The African Image*, "To us in multi-racial
communities, then, *negritude* is just so much intellectual

talk, a cult" (p. 40). And later: "If there is any *negritude* in the black man's art in South Africa, it is because we *are* African. If a writer's tone is healthy, he is bound to express the African in him. Stripped of Senghor's philosophic musings, the African traits he speaks of can be taken for granted: they are social anthropology" (p. 53).

On the other hand, for Thomas Melone, of Cameroon, negritude is "the language of the Negro-African conscience." Earlier in his monograph on the subject,[51] he claims that it "gives an answer to the Negro world in its agonizing search for its own image." This brings us back again to the question of identity, which enables the black man to know himself, his past, his present, and his future potential. In its revolutionary manifestations—Sartre has called it "the only great revolutionary poetry of our day"[52] —it also challenges the conscience of the white man.

Taking the white man's language, dislocating his syntax, recharging his words with new strength and sometimes with new meaning before hurling them back in his teeth, while upsetting his self-righteous complacency and clichés, our poets rehabilitate such terms as Africa and blackness, beauty and peace. Take "nègre" for example, a harsh word, hard on the ear and even harder on the nerves, a target for generations of European contempt. These writers, though doubtless preferring to be called "Africains" or "Noirs," deliberately adopt "Negritude" as the name of their movement and sponsor in 1966 the "First World Festival of *Negro* Arts" (italics mine). No longer can "Négro-Afri-

51. *De la Négritude dans la littérature négro-africaine;* the quotations are from pp. 128 and 17.
52. See Sartre's preface to the 1948 Senghor anthology, p. xii. Quaison-Sackey, in *Africa Unbound*, also stresses the revolutionary aspect of the African Personality.

cain" be considered a symbol of shame. Thus the critic who dismisses a part of Damas's *Black Label* as "defiant nonsense" may have missed the psychological justification for such lines as:

> The White will never be Negro
> For beauty is Negro
> and Negro is wisdom
> for endurance is Negro
> and Negro is courage
> for patience is Negro
> and Negro is irony[53]

In the main, the negritude revolution is a nonviolent one. As victims of racism, Black Africans know they have been sinned against, they denounce injustice, but they look forward to a new kind of world in which exploitation, war, and colonialism will become anachronisms. Perhaps this assurance stems largely from the knowledge that, as the overwhelming majority in their countries, Black Africans have time on their side. In any event, their works express surprisingly little hatred and an astonishing propensity to pardon past offenses. In a poem honoring African comrades killed in World War II, Senghor pleads: "Black martyrs, O immortal race, give me leave to say the words that will forgive."[54] Years later Tchicaya U Tam'si, of Congo Brazzaville, agrees to overlook "my blood on their hands" and to forgive the whites, provided "they leave me to be Congolese in peace."[55]

53. In Moore, *Seven African Writers*, p. xx. As an example of another poem similar to that of Damas in its insistent repetition of the word "nègre," see Martial Sinda, *Premier chant du départ* (Paris, 1956), p. 43.

54. Senghor, *Poèmes*, p. 77.

55. U Tam'si, *Epitomé*, p. 54.

African unity and African socialism are too important in contemporary African thinking to be overlooked in a discussion of African literature. Both are ideals, almost universally professed on that continent but no more immediately attainable than France's Liberty, Equality, Fraternity; Russia's Dictatorship of the Proletariat; or the truths that the Founding Fathers held to be self-evident. Both African unity and African socialism have inspired innumerable statements by political and intellectual leaders. On the need for unity, there is unanimity, while the socialism has provoked some difference of opinion. Most agree, however, that some type of socialism is necessary to start their countries on the road to economic and social progress.[56] In almost every instance, the traditional communalism is cited as a natural forerunner of socialism and, in most cases, the term *African* is used to indicate a firm intention not to import bodily and uncritically the socialism of any other state.

When the late Senator John F. Kennedy declared in June 1959, "Whatever one's point of view, one fact cannot be denied—the future of Africa will seriously affect, for better or worse, the future of the United States," I doubt that even he could have foreseen the impact that militant African writers would exert on black American militants. Perhaps he could have anticipated Nkrumah's attack on American investment in South Africa, for that had already been criticized here at home. But could he have predicted

56. Cf. W. H. Friedland and C. G. Rosberg, Jr., *African Socialism* (Stanford University Press, 1964). This volume includes comments on African socialism by numerous African leaders. See also L. S. Senghor, *On African Socialism* (New York: Praeger, 1964); Republic of Kenya, *African Socialism and Its Application to Planning in Kenya* (1965).

that a theoretician of the Algerian revolution would prepare a blueprint that some of our young people seem to be
following religiously? Could Kennedy have forecast that
his own murder would be cited by a Nigerian novelist to
illustrate that values are relative and constantly changing?
"Take the United States which is the most powerful country in the so-called Free World and whose constitution has
inspired many a movement for equality and freedom. Does
freedom there mean the same thing for everyone? For the
late J. F. Kennedy and for the school children who shouted
'we are free' when they heard of his assassination or their
elders who celebrated with champagne?"[57] Could Kennedy
have foreseen that in 1964 three young Africans would
write a book entitled *Les Noirs aux Etats-Unis pour les
Africains*, with photographs of a Negro youth being attacked by a Birmingham policeman and police dog, and a
young black girl being manhandled by two of Birmingham's Finest? The authors review the history of the Afro-
American, discuss his organizations—NAACP, SCLC,
SNCC, and the Black Muslims (which they prefer)—and
conclude that the African should have no illusions about
cooperation with the Western world:

As far as Africa is concerned, we have often heard that it has
no capital, and this is why development is difficult. We have
often heard that one cannot develop a country, or raise the
African's standard of living in a century. We say, however,
that black Americans have been living with white Americans
for four centuries—since the arrival of the first European
settlers—America was born, built, and became prosperous

57. From a lecture delivered by Chinua Achebe in April 1964.
Quoted from Barbara Nolen's *Africa Is People* (New York: E. P.
Dutton, 1967), p. 180.

thanks to the black man's labor—nevertheless, America's black masses are stagnating in ignorance, illiteracy, insecurity, filth, disease.

In view of these facts, it is certain that African development will never come with the consent and support of the Western World, for the simple reason that African development means the retrogression of European development.[58]

Summing up this once-over-lightly and necessarily incomplete survey of revolutionary African literature, we have seen something of the early background when journalists, lawyers, and pastors were arguing for African values and a share in government. As a shortcut to an acquaintance with some of Africa's poets and novelists, I have based my presentation on their search for identity, negritude, the African personality, and their ironical treatment of Civilization. Throughout this paper I have quoted abundantly, convinced that in a discussion of African literature, as in matters political, social, and economic, the African must be allowed to speak for himself. In the main, statements by the Africans seem to me less extreme and violent than many by West Indian and North American blacks. I know of no work so impassioned as Claude McKay's unforgettable sonnet, "If We Must Die," which exhorts ". . . we must meet the common foe! / Though far outnumbered let us show us brave, / And for their thousand blows deal one deathblow!" But here I am trespassing on territory allocated to my distinguished colleague.

58. N'Diaye, Bassane, and Poyas, *Les Noirs aux Etats-Unis pour les Africains*, p. 175.

Bibliography

The works listed below are those cited or quoted in my text. I have not attempted to compile here a comprehensive bibliography of African literature.

Abrahams, Peter. *Return to Goli.* London: Faber & Faber, 1953.
———. *A Wreath for Udomo.* London: Faber & Faber, 1956.
Achebe, Chinua. *A Man of the People.* London: Heinemann, 1966.
———. *No Longer at Ease.* London: Heinemann, 1960.
———. *Things Fall Apart.* London: Heinemann, 1958.
Allen, Samuel W. "Negritude and Its Relevance to the American Negro Writer." In *The American Negro Writer and His Roots.* New York: AMSAC, 1960.
Azikiwe, Nnamdi. *Renascent Africa.* Accra: The Author, 1937.
Badian, Seydou. *Sous l'orage.* Paris: Présence Africaine, 1963.
Bebey, Francis. *Le Fils d'Agatha Moudio.* Yaoundé: Editions CLE, 1967.
Beti, Mongo. *Mission terminée.* Paris: Editions Corréa, 1957.
———. *Le pauvre Christ de Bomba.* Paris: Laffont, 1956.
———. *Ville cruelle.* Paris: Présence Africaine, n.d. (Published under the nom de plume Eza Boto.)
Césaire, Aimé. *Cahier d'un retour au pays natal.* New York: Brentano's, 1947.
———. *Discours sur le colonialisme.* Paris: Présence Africaine, 1955.
———. *Une Saison au Congo:* Paris: Présence Africaine, 1966.

Clark, J. P. *America, Their America*. London: André Deutsch, 1964.

Conton, William. *The African*. Boston: Little, Brown, 1960.

Dadié, Bernard. *Climbié*. Paris: Seghers, 1956.

———. *Un Nègre à Paris*. Paris: Présence Africaine, 1959.

———. *Patron de New-York*. Paris: Présence Africaine, 1964.

Damas, Léon G. *Black Label*. Paris: Gallimard, 1956.

———. *Pigments*. Paris: G.L.M., 1937; Présence Africaine, 1962.

Dempster, Roland Tombekai. "Africa's Plea." In Hughes, *Poems from Black Africa*.

Dia, Amadou Cissé. *Les derniers jours de Lat Dior*. Paris: Présence Africaine, 1966.

Diakhaté, Lamine. *Temps de mémoire*. Paris: Présence Africaine, 1967.

Diallo, Assane. "Blues." In *Nouvelle Somme de poésie du monde noir*. Paris: Présence Africaine, 1966.

Dike, K. O., and others. *Eminent Nigerians of the Nineteenth Century*. Cambridge University Press, 1960. (A series of studies originally broadcast by the Nigerian Broadcasting Corporation.)

Diop, Birago. *Contes d'Amadou Koumba*. Paris: Fasquelle, 1947.

———. *Nouveaux Contes d'Amadou Koumba*. Paris: Présence Africaine, 1958.

Diop, David. *Coups de Pilon*. Paris: Présence Africaine, 1961. The translation of "The Vultures" is found in Moore and Beier, *Modern Poetry from Africa*.

Ekwensi, Cyprian. *Beautiful Feathers*. London: Hutchinson, 1963.

———. *People of the City*. London: Andrew Dakers, 1954.

Fanon, Frantz. *The Wretched of the Earth*. New York: Grove Press, 1966.

Gatheru, R. Mugo. *Child of Two Worlds*. New York: Doubleday Anchor, 1965.

Gide, André. *Voyage au Congo*. Paris: Gallimard, 1927.

Gordimer, Nadine, and Lionel Abrahams, eds. *South African Writing Today*. London: Penguin, 1967.

Grégoire, Abbé Henri. *De la Littérature des Nègres*. Paris: Chez Maradan, 1808.

Hama, Boubou. *Enquête sur les fondements et la genèse de l'unité africaine*. Paris: Présence Africaine, 1966.

Hodgkin, Thomas. *Nationalism in Colonial Africa*. London: Frederick Muller, 1956.

Hughes, Langston, ed. *Poems from Black Africa*. Bloomington: Indiana University Press, 1963.

Hutchinson, Alfred. *Road to Ghana*. London: Gollancz, 1960.

Jabavu, Nona. *The Ochre People*. London: John Murray, 1963.

July, Robert W. *The Origins of Modern African Thought*. New York: Praeger, 1967.

Kane, Cheikh Hamidou. *L'Aventure ambiguë*. Paris: Julliard, 1962.

Kenyatta, Jomo. *Facing Mount Kenya*. London: Secker and Warburg, 1938.

Laye, Camara. *Dramouss*. Paris: Plon, 1966.

———. *L'Enfant noir*. Paris: Plon, 1953. (Translated as *The African Child*.)

———. *Le Regard du roi*. Paris: Plon, 1954. (Translated as *The Radiance of the King*.)

Loba, Aké. *Kocoumbo, l'étudiant noir*. Paris: Flammarion, 1960.

Maran, René. *Batouala*. Edition définitive. Paris: Albin Michel, 1938. (First published and awarded the Goncourt Prize in 1921.)

Mboya, Tom. *Freedom and After*. Boston: Little, Brown, 1963.

Melone, Thomas. *De la Négritude dans la littérature négro-africaine.* Paris: Présence Africaine, 1962.

Mofolo, Thomas. *Chaka.* Basutoland, 1925; English trans., London: Oxford University Press, 1931; French version, Paris: Gallimard, 1940.

Moore, Gerald. *Seven African Writers.* London: Oxford University Press, 1962.

Moore, Gerald, and Ulli Beier. *Modern Poetry from Africa.* London: Penguin, 1963.

Mphahlele, Ezekiel. *The African Image.* London: Faber & Faber, 1962.

——. *Down Second Avenue.* London: Faber & Faber, 1959.

N'Diaye, Bassane, and Poyas. *Les Noirs aux Etats-Unis, pour les Africains.* Paris: Réalités Africaines, 1964.

Ngugi, James. *A Grain of Wheat.* London: Heinemann, 1968.

Niang, Lamine. *Négristique.* Paris: Présence Africaine, 1963.

Nicol, Davidson. "The Continent That Lies within Us." In Hughes, *Poems from Black Africa.*

Nkosi, Lewis. "Black Power or Souls of Black Writers." In Gordimer and Abrahams, *South African Writing Today.* Originally published in Nkosi's *Home and Exile.* London: Longmans, Green, 1965.

Nkrumah, Kwame. *I Speak of Freedom.* New York: Praeger, 1961.

Nzekwu, Onuora. *Wand of Noble Wood.* London: Hutchinson, 1961.

Okara, Gabriel. "Once upon a time." In Hughes, *Poems from Black Africa.*

Oulogucm, Yambo. "A mon mari." In *Nouvelle Somme de poésie du monde noir.* Paris: Présence Africaine, 1966. (His first novel, *Le Devoir de violence* [Paris: Seuil, 1968] was recently awarded the Renaudot prize.)

Ousmane, Sembène. *Les Bouts de bois de Dieu.* Paris: Le Livre Contemporain, 1960. (Translated as *God's Bits of Wood.* New York: Doubleday, 1963.)

———. *O Pays mon beau peuple.* Paris: Le Livre Contemporain, 1957.

Oyono, Ferdinand. *Chemin d'Europe.* Paris: Julliard, 1960.

———. *Une Vie de boy.* Paris: Julliard, 1956. (Translated as *Houseboy.* London: Heinemann, 1966.)

———. *Le vieux nègre et la médaille.* Paris: Julliard, 1956. (Translated as *The Old Man and the Medal.* London: Heinemann, 1968.)

Philombe, René. "Civilisation." In Lilyan Lagneau, ed., *Neuf Poètes camerounais.* Yaoundé: Editions CLE, 1965.

Quaison-Sackey, Alex. *Africa Unbound.* New York: Praeger, 1963.

Say, Bania Mahamadou. "Lapsus." In *Le Niger.* Niamey, July 15, 1968.

Senghor, Léopold Sédar. *Anthologie de la nouvelle poésie nègre et malgache.* Paris: Presses Universitaires de France, 1948.

———. "Ce que l'homme noir apporte." In *L'Homme de Couleur.* Paris: Plon, 1939.

———. "Chaka" and "Prayer for Peace." In Senghor's *Selected Poems,* trans. John Reed and Clive Wake. New York: Atheneum, 1964.

———. *Chants d'ombre.* Paris: Seuil, 1945.

———. *Liberté I, Négritude et Humanisme.* Paris: Seuil, 1964. (Essays, prefaces, and speeches)

———. "New-York." In *Ethiopiques.* Paris: Seuil, 1956. Trans. in Moore and Beier, *Modern Poetry from Africa.*

———. *Poèmes.* Paris: Seuil, 1964.

Socé, Ousmane. *Contes et légendes d'Afrique Noire.* Paris: Nouvelles Editions Latines, 1962.

Socé, Ousmane. *Mirages de Paris*. Paris: Nouvelles Editions Latines, 1955.

Soyinka, Wole. *The Interpreters*. London: André Deutsch, 1965.

———. *The Lion and the Jewel*. London: Oxford University Press, 1963.

———. "Telephone Conversation." In Moore and Beier, *Modern Poetry from Africa*.

Touré, Sékou. *L'Expérience guinéenne et l'unité africaine*. Paris: Présence Africaine, 1959.

Tutuola, Amos. *The Palm Wine Drinkard*. London: Faber & Faber, 1952.

U Tam'si, Tchicaya. *Epitomé*. Tunis: Société Nationale d'Edition, 1962.

Wade, Abdoulaye. "Afrique Noire et Union Française." In *Les Etudiants noirs parlent*. Paris: Présence Africaine, 1952.

Wade, Amadou Moustapha. "Les 'Civilisateurs'." In *Les Etudiants noirs parlent*. Paris: Présence Africaine, 1952.

"Survival Motion"
A Study of the Black Writer
and the Black Revolution
in America

STEPHEN E. HENDERSON

THE term "militant" when applied to black people in the United States is at once inadequate and redundant; when applied to black writers it circumscribes them in a way which they themselves reject. Black writers are "militant" only to white people and to Negroes who think "white," for merely to say, "I'm black," in the United States is an act of resistance; to say out loud, "I'm black and I'm proud"[1] is an act of rebellion; to attempt systematically to move black people to act out of their beauty and their blackness in white America is to foment revolution. To write black poetry is an act of survival, of regeneration, of love. Black writers do not write for white people and refuse to be judged by them. They write for black people and they write about their blackness, and out of their blackness, rejecting anyone and anything that stands in the way of self-knowledge and self-celebration. They know that to assert blackness in America is to be "militant," to be dangerous, to be subversive, to be revolutionary, and they know this in a way that even the Harlem Renaissance did not. The poets and the playwrights are especially articulate and especially relevant and speak directly to the people.

1. Cf. James Brown's rhythm-and-blues song, "Say It Loud—I'm Black and I'm Proud."

For this reason I have centered my remarks, fragmentary as they are, upon them.

Originally, this paper was to have been entitled "The Role of the Black Writer in America in Revolution," but a little reflection indicated to me the necessity of limiting the topic in a way which would not presume too much upon my own personal beliefs on one hand and the credulity of my audience on the other. One could seriously question, for example, that *America* in any meaningful sense of the term is in a state of "revolution." And even assuming that the country were in such a general state of "revolution," one could question whether the black writer has any special obligation to that general revolution. Indeed, with the cutback in foreign aid, with the recent enactment of a puerile gun-control law, with the duplicity on the question of open housing, with the spineless ignoring of the recommendations of the Kerner Commission, with the sentencing of Dr. Spock and Professor Coffin, with the continual harassment of black political leaders, with the murder of Robert Kennedy and Martin Luther King, with the strength shown by George Wallace in the Presidential campaign, and the nascent threat of Ronald Reagan, one wonders instead whether the country is in a state of reactionary convulsion, brought about by its head-on confrontation with the reality of blackness and its own spiritual bankruptcy.

Thus, it seems to me closer to the truth, when speaking generally of the present situation in this country, to speak of resistance and rebellion: white resistance to change and black resistance to oppression, and rebellion by the young and the poor and the black against a repressive social and economic order which for centuries, to return to my theme, has kept the vast majority of black people in a state of economic and social and political subjection. Despite these qualifications, however, one knows that there is a

revolutionary consciousness in this country which em-
braces especially the poor, and the young, and the black.
My task, however, is not to talk about those groups in any
separate sense, although the young do, indeed, grow older
and move to the suburbs; but the poor quite often remain
poor; the poor more often than not are black; and, of
course, the black remain black. The point of this entire
discussion is that the real revolution which is occurring in
America today is the Black Consciousness Movement, the
transfiguration of blackness, a necessary first stage in the
liberation of black people, and conceivably of all Americans.

The news media have called attention to the more obvious aspects of the black rebellion—the cities on fire, the
alleged sniping, the bomb plots, the militant organizations,
the charismatic leaders. But until recently, with the CBS
series "Of Black America," for example, they have paid
little attention to—indeed, apparently have failed to grasp
—the fact that a profound revolution is occurring in the
minds of black people and that when that revolution is
complete (and there is nothing to stop it save sheer annihi-
lation)—when it is complete, when these Negroes have
been turned into black people, conscious and whole and
powerful and proud, the revolution will have become ex-
ternalized, and the United States as a country will either be
transformed or destroyed.

It is, perhaps, pointless to talk about *how* the transformation will take place. Such talk usually resolves itself into the
question of violence versus nonviolence, which means,
more often than not, whether black people would defend
themselves if attacked. But that should no longer be a
question in anyone's mind. The question of violence now is
no longer *if* but *how;* that is to say, not whether black
people would defend themselves *if* attacked; not whether

they would be willing to die for freedom and manhood and decency, but *how* they would defend themselves, how they would fight for that freedom; not whether they would be subjected to violence, for we know now (though not to the full extent) that this country has been built upon violence, physical, mental, and spiritual—by the virtual extermination of the Indian, by the enslavement of the African, and the systematic degradation of his progeny in America. The question is not *if* but *how*. In a way this has always been the question, but because it has either been quietly forgotten, or ignored, or distorted, or phrased in irrelevant or sophistic terms, we have come up with partial answers, partial truths.

Not—the question is not, in a word, whether America is capable of genocide; not *whether* the white man would exterminate the black (if he could), but *how*. This question of violence is not *whether* the black man would defend himself, but *how*, and against what. The question is thus refined to the mode of the attack. If the attack were physical (and it has been physical), then we would get laws to protect us. And we have obtained such laws. And if the laws themselves were used as weapons against us? Then we would shatter those unjust laws with Soul Force, with our spirituals and our dirges and our sorrow songs. Margaret Walker speaks for us:

> For my people everywhere singing their slave songs repeatedly: their dirges and their ditties and their blues and jubilees, praying their prayers nightly to an unknown god, bending their knees humbly to an unseen power.[2]

2. From "For My People," in *American Negro Poetry*, ed. Arna Bontemps (New York: Hill & Wang, 1963), p. 128.

And there emerged among us a great and powerful spirit, and he galvanized his people and shook the conscience of the nation. But this nation has a seemingly endless capacity for self-deception; it tires easily from moral confrontation; and by the time that Dr. King was proposing his Poor People's Campaign the nation which four years earlier had thrilled to his golden voice, which had *dreamt* his dream, was now awake and peevish, and warned this man of peace of violence. And so he went up to the mountain to pray, and he saw his God and he saw the glory and he saw the promised land. And when he came down to tell the good news, the dream was "exploded down his throat." And the shock and the anger that we felt. The disbelief. A few rumbles from the ghettoes. The pious voices. The instant deification by the mass media, by the political establishment.

Wait until after the funeral!

We waited.

The terrible tension in Atlanta, fearful for its image. The students trooping through the drizzling rain. The sirens. The five fire-bombed stores. The funeral cortege. The governor hiding in the capitol, cracking jokes about coons. The prurient cameras. The popinjays. My college. The boasting. The funeral has brought us to the mainstream of American life. Yes, the mainstream, choked with the bodies of the dead—the President and the prophet, and Malcolm, and gentle Medgar Evers, and all the bodies of all the dead selves that daily die from compromise and corruption and moral imbecility. The mainstream choked with all the filth and trivia of our lives—the endless cheap mementoes, the banners, the plaques, the medallions, the chapels, the schools, the records. The mainstream of American life, where we shatter a President's mind into a million silver coins and reduce a living man (a prophet of peace, a man of God) to a tawdry American saint.

And what is the relevance? And what is the role of the black writer amidst all of this national death? Black writers have spoken individually and collectively and eloquently for themselves, so I don't presume to speak for them, rather about them. So I say first that the relevance is that King was a poet and a prophet and a mediator. He was tolerated and respected by the American political establishment, both local and national, in a way that Malcolm was not, and he moved us, like Malcolm, with the consummate language of the Black Experience. Yet he had a dream "exploded down his throat." Soul Force was met with brute force.

There was logic behind this, of course, the logic we have always known: The question was and *is* the question of survival, not *if*, but *how*. Not a question of violence. We know that all too well. A young black poet, Don L. Lee, puts it this way:

> When I was 17
> I didn't have time to dream,
> Dreams didn't exist—
> Prayers did, as dreams.
> I am now 17 & 8.
> I still don't dream.
> Father forgive us for we know what we do.

The question is survival, and the poet says:

> i ain't seen no poems stop a .38,
> i ain't seen no stanzas break a honkie's head,
> i ain't seen no metaphors stop a tank.[3]

3. Both excerpts are from "In the Interest of Black Salvation," in *Black Pride* (Detroit: Broadside Press, 1968), p. 21.

And so to some extent the role of the black writer as writer is irrelevant, for if the final confrontation is physical, then the writer's obligation will be the same as everyone else's —to have his dream "exploded down his throat" or to protect himself and his family and his people by whatever means possible. However, no one can predict the time of confrontation, even if it is to be physical, and certainly no black man or woman deludes himself or herself that a massive use of force against them is impossible, for we have all seen the prelude in a hundred cities; we have seen the justification by the press; we have decoded the "niggerkill" behind the current political jargon. We know what it means, not only in our cities but on our campuses where sensitive people of all colors and classes deplore an unjust war abroad and vested irrelevance at home. So alongside Harlem and Chicago, and Cleveland and Detroit and Atlanta, we must place Berkeley and Howard and Columbia and Tuskegee and Clafflin and South Carolina State College and Fisk.

—I remember, I said, the terrible tension in Atlanta the night Dr. King was murdered, the endless sirens and the patrol cars. I remember the constant surveillance and the newspaper statement of a young colleague: "There's nothing revolutionary going on here but the curriculum." Indeed. Nothing *but* the curriculum! The *proper* curriculum would have prepared young black people to assess themselves and their country with some degree of sanity and balance, would have saved them from the ghoulish trading on this good man's death. Black poets could have told them; black poets could have warned them; black poets could have saved them from the "mainstream." And black poets tried after his death, as they had tried after Malcolm's death, to prepare them for the impending confrontation which now no one doubts. The only question is whether the violence is to be physical or a heightened form of the intellectual and spiritual arrogance which masquerades as integration and which has assaulted us, in one form or another, for nearly four hundred years. Black writers, but especially black poets, can save us, all of us, from this strange disease, for the Movement is secular now. Our poets are now our prophets. They have come to baptize us in blackness, to inform us with Soul.

This baptism in blackness comprises two distinct elements which especially animate the recent pattern of black writing, although they were crystallized in many works of the Harlem Renaissance. They are (1) the rejection of white middle-class cultural values and (2) the affirmation of black selfhood, or, depending on the intensity of the writer's involvement, (*a*) the destruction of anything that stands in the way of selfhood and (*b*) a celebration of blackness. Another feature, a variation of *a*, is preëmptive attack, a kind of intellectual guerrilla warfare, which may range all the way from "letters to the editor" to the systematic rejection of and attack upon William Styron's *Confessions of Nat Turner* in a series of crackling essays by some of the most talented of contemporary black writers.[4]

Lerone Bennett, historian and senior editor of *Ebony* magazine, is one of ten black writers who were outraged by the Styron portraiture of Nat Turner. Bennett declares:

> The voice in this confession is the voice of William Styron.
> The images are the images of William Styron.
> The confession is the confession of William Styron.
> And Styron's *Confessions*, despite the revealing hosannas of

4. See *William Styron's Nat Turner: Ten Black Writers Respond*, ed. John H. Clarke (Boston: Beacon Press, 1968).

the white culture structure, is a record of the hallucinatory silence of our history, of 350 years "of talk buried deep in dreams." Styron *dreams*, but he refuses to confront history and that refusal defines his book which tells us little about the historical Nat Turner and a great deal about William Styron and the white culture structure which made the book a modern literary happening.

Styron tells us he is meditating on history. But we are not fooled. We know that he is really trying to escape history. We know—he confesses it—that he is trying to escape the judgment of history embodied in Nat Turner and his spiritual sons of the twentieth century. ("Nat's Last White Man," in *Ten Black Writers Respond*, p. 4.)

Bennett then proceeds to contrast the impact made by the historical Nat Turner upon Thomas Gray, his racist recorder, and the liberal William Styron.

The difference in tone between the *Confessions* of Gray, the racist, and Styron the white liberal, gives one pause. Gray, who loathed Nat but who looked into his eyes, gives him to history unrepentant, courageous, sure of his act and his eventual vindication. Styron, who says he sympathizes with Nat, destroys him as a man and as a leader. And the terrifying implication of this fact is that the fascination-horror of a bigot may be more compelling than the fascination-anxiety of a white liberal. (*Ibid.*, p. 16.)

Two of the essays which most provoked the white establishment were those by Vincent Harding, professor of history at Spelman College, and Mike Thelwell, instructor of English at the University of Massachusetts. Grudgingly, the critics praise both of these men. In his review-article in

The New York Review of Books (Sept. 12, 1968, pp.
34–37), Eugene Genovese, after dismissing the other writers as essentially repetitious and inaccurate, singles out
Harding and Thelwell as "gifted," and then prepares to
defuse what they have to say by calling to question the
validity of the book that most of the writers cited, Herbert
Aptheker's *American Negro Slave Revolts* (Columbia University Press, 1945). In a review of *Ten Black Writers
Respond*, in *The New York Times Book Review* (Aug.
11, 1968), Martin Duberman takes a similar tack. *Time*
magazine (July 12, 1968) makes the work essentially a
fabrication or wish fulfillment on the part of the black
writers involved; but a serious reading of the volume indicates that the writers raise many questions which their
white critics have not fully answered. Harding's essay on
the subject hardly receives the credit that it deserves, nor
does Kaiser's; and though the lame justifications of Styron's
historical distortions, by both the author himself and his
apologists, have some theoretical merit, they do not come to
grips with the central problem; for, if anything, the writing
of Styron's book was a political gesture, albeit a muddled
one; and on that point alone the author invited the kind of
attack he received. At any rate, one can be fairly certain
that the next white writer will think twice before presum-
ing to interpret the Black Experience.[5] Thus the whole
syndrome of the novel and the responses marks an important change in the American literary climate; it marks a

    5. Since I wrote this (Oct. 1968), sharply critical reviews of
L. Neal's and LeRoi Jones's *Black Fire* suggest that the problem of
"interpretation" is still very much with us. See Jack Richardson's
review, "The Black Arts," *The New York Review of Books*,
Dec. 19, 1968, pp. 10–13; Peter Berek's "Using Black Magic with
the Word on the World," *Saturday Review*, Nov. 30, 1968, pp.
35–37; and Charles R. Larson, *ibid.*, pp. 37–38.

new coming of age of the black literary intellectual. It will
not be soon forgotten, for this is just the beginning of a
systematic attempt to "tell it like it is"—in the words of
Lerone Bennett again, "to wrest the Negro image from
white control."[6]

This rejection of white values and standards is one of the
most powerful aspects of the black revolution. It appears in
fiction, in drama, in poetry, and in criticism, both literary
and social, when such distinctions are admitted. It is directed not only at whites but at Negroes too, who have
rejected their blackness or have never been fully aware of
it.

Here are two bitter repudiations of the white values
which, as in Styron, deliberately cannibalize the meaning of
the black man's life. In the first poem, by Sonia Sanchez,
the "Righteous Brothers" are a duo of white singers who
have become rich and famous for their skilful imitations of
black singers, while the men like Al Hibbler and Roy
Hamilton whose voices they stole have relatively little pop-
ularity today.

> to/blk/record/buyers
>
> don't play me no
> righteous bros.
>   white people
> ain't right bout nothing
> no mo'.
>   don't tell me bout
> foreign dudes
>   cuz no blk/
> people are grooving on a
> sunday afternoon.

6. *The Negro Mood* (New York: Ballantine Books, 1965), p. 92.

```
                    they either
         making out/
                    signifying/
                              drinking/
         making molotov cocktails/
                              stealing/
         or rather taking their goods
         from the honky thieves who
         ain't hung up
                    on no pacifist/jesus
                         cross.          but.
         play blk/songs
                    to drown out the
         shit/screams of honkies.     AAAH.
         AAAH.    AAAH.    yeah.    brothers.
         andmanymoretogo.⁷
```

In a poem entitled "The Black Narrator: At a Symposium for Afro-Americans,"⁸ Le Graham, a Detroit poet,
dramatizes the effect of white values upon creative black
minds, and shouts his own black beauty in his own black
language.

1

White poems
are daggers. guns. cops.
                    piercing hearts in weird design. Ofays
                    beating niggers to their knees. Coloured
                    girls with wigs passing & cutting Afro's
                    mind. Or black poems judged by whitey's
                    standards. 11:45 & still no ring (eastern
standard time. owned by grey cats on mainline U.S.A.)

7. Quoted from the *Liberator*, Vol. 8, No. 7 (July 1968), p. 10.
8. See *The Black Narrator* (broadsheet, copyright by author,
1966), pp. 5, 6.

These poems are such things. pointed. like twist drills
                                   parting tools. I know
the creator
                (in classroom faces. human relationship meetings
morning greetings as a habit. a state of mind after a work-
shop on blackism)

2

Black poems are beautiful
egyptian princesses. afro-americans. john o. killens. ossie
                                davis. leroi jones. mal
                                colm x shabazz. robert
                                williams. lumumba. A
poem for wooly-haired brothers. natural-haired sisters.
Bimbos. boots & woogies. Or nappy-headed youngsters
                     Cause they want what i
                     want: blood from revolutions. A
                           fast boat to Africa. ghana
                           the cameroons uganda &
                           nigeria . . .

3

Here in america i want black thoughts. in forms of con
crete skies
tumbling down
on dingy ofays. on negro
middleclass heads (konked-haired hipsters. wig-wearing
       whores. sophisticated teachers. inspiring professors
       . . . schooled in propaganda)
Crush their minds & lives thoughts. Talk to them in chinese
                                        vietnamese
                                   or
                           black language

Fuck their minds up. cross-cut & rip-saw
their ideas. in
ugly design. improper
balance. Yeah.
using black primitive standards.

There should be no doubt in anyone's mind that these
poems were not intended for white readers and white audiences, that their purpose was direct address to the black
community, to get us together to TCB. If there is any
doubt in anyone's mind, Don L. Lee dispels it. He states
that his poetry is not directed to "white boys and girls" but
to black people. Nor is he writing for "National Book
Awards and Pulitzer prizes," but for his people. They and
they alone can judge what he has written. His poetry
speaks for them and to them—to "the man with the wine
bottle and processed hair"—about rat-infested slums and
the spiritual corruption they breed. His poetry is a weapon
for his people at the same time that it draws upon them for
strength. It is "like daggers, broken brew bottles, bullets,
swift razors from black hands cutting through slum land-
lords and Negro dope pushers." It will confront "pimps
and prostitutes and aid in the destruction of their actions."
He says, "Black poems are a part of the people: An energy
source for the people's life style."[9]

A survey of the attitudes of representative black writers
was recently conducted by Hoyt Fuller, the urbane, articulate managing editor of *Negro Digest*.[10] Three of the ques-

9. The quotations are from a speech at the University of Wisconsin, Madison, Aug. 9, 1968; later printed in *Negro Digest*
(Sept./Oct. 1968), pp. 27–32.
10. The findings were published in the January 1968 issue of
Negro Digest; parenthetical page numbers in the text refer to this
issue.

tions asked required the writer to indicate whether he believed in a "black Aesthetic," whether the black writer
should consciously and deliberately seek to explore the
Black Experience, and whether he should address his work
to black audiences. The response was varied, but the drift,
especially among the younger writers, was in the direction
of Don L. Lee. For example, the gifted Conrad Kent
Rivers, who died this year at age thirty-four, declared: "If
we fail to write for black people, we—in effect—fail to
write at all" (p. 17). Mari Evans broadened the perspective: "Some things should be said at home and some in the
marketplace. Black writers should decide whether what
they have to say *needs* to be said to white or black folks and
attempt to market their work accordingly. There are some
other things whitey needs to be told—and some things the
brother needs to hear" (p. 22).

Perhaps the most controversial aspect of this position on
the audience, and the one most unsettling to whites, is the
insistence that, despite the proliferation of "experts," whites
are unable to evaluate the Black Experience, and, conse-
quently, any work of art derived from it or addressed to
those who live it. Laurence Neal goes deeper: the white
critic is irrelevant to his concern, except that the dead hand
of his influence must be kept off the black poem.

This is the issue finally. We must determine, for ourselves, what
is good literature (art) and what is bad. We cannot abdicate
our culture to those who exist outside of us. We should guard
and protect our culture viciously, and work critical ju-ju on
those who screw up. (p. 83)

Using a figure drawn from the jazz experience, Neal calls
upon black writers to emulate the vision of Parker, Coltrane, Cecil Taylor:

Open up, Black writers. Open up. Blow. Yeah, blow those white dreams and demons away. Kill the beast of a fetid literary tradition. Blow them away. Open up. Link up with the struggle. Confront yourselves. Do your thing whenever and wherever you can. Talk to each other. Your own magazines and journals. Your own films and playhouses. Your own critique. White writers can teach you very little. Perhaps some precise kind of technique. But Stevie Wonder's technique is finally hipper than T. S. Eliot's. Talk to each other. No alienation in white liberal zones. Embrace black people; experiment with Black styles. What, for example, is the meaning of the boogaloo? I mean it. James Brown is the best poet we got baby. (pp. 83–84)

And if there is any doubt that black writers are able to "work critical ju-ju," the pages of *Liberator, The Journal of Black Poetry, Black Dialogue,* and *Negro Digest* should blow it away. *Ten Black Writers Respond* served formal notice of the territorial imperative.

In the theatre the same independence asserts itself. Two of the central figures are LeRoi Jones and his protégé, Ed Bullins, while among many talented actors one must certainly mention Ossie Davis. It is not an accident that Le Graham includes the two older men in his catalogue of heroes. Jones's pioneering work in the Black Arts Theatre in New York opened the minds of black theatre people all over the country. His justly famous play, *The Dutchman,* is a convulsive rejection of sexual stereotypes and is a good indicator of his dramatic power. Some years ago he wrote about his concept of theatre: "The Revolutionary Theatre should force change, it should be change. If the beautiful see themselves, they will know themselves."[11] The words

11. LeRoi Jones, in *The New York Times,* Oct. 1, 1968, Sec. C, p. 49.

are reminiscent of an earlier cultural revolutionary, Waring
Cuney, who wrote in 1926, while a student at Lincoln
University, a poem that has received wide acclaim. It is
entitled "No Images."

> She does not know
> Her beauty,
> She thinks her brown body
> Has no glory.
>
> If she could dance
> Naked,
> Under palm trees
> And see her image in the river
> She would know.
>
> But there are no palm trees
> On the street,
> And dishwater gives back no images.
>
> *(American Negro Poetry*, pp. 98–99)

The new Black Arts *make* the dishwater give back the
images of black beauty; and Ed Bullins, who recently
turned down a Hollywood offer to do a screenplay from
one of his works, describes his intent as a playwright: "I
write for black people," he states in words identical to
those of Don L. Lee and other young writers, "to enter-
tain, to instruct, to help."[12] He believes in taking his art *to*
his people in street-corner theatre, "where the pimps,
whores and hustlers and the black working class are." He is
not concerned with Broadway, just as the poets are not

12. This and other comments on the Black Theatre are from
The New York Times, Oct. 1, 1968, Sec. C, p. 49. See also the
special issue on the Black Theatre in *The Drama Review*, Vol. 12,
No. 4 (Summer 1968); Bullins was special editor for this issue.
See also April 1966, 1967, 1968 issues of *Negro Digest*.

concerned with National Book Awards and Pulitzer prizes. Indeed, it is obvious that if Styron's novel could win a Pulitzer prize in 1967 it did so because it reflected a set of cultural values which the black writer rejects, values which Frantz Fanon calls the "Mediterranean values" of the Graeco-Roman tradition.

Black actors are equally engaged. Barbara Ann Teer, who is also a director, says of her acting that she is trying to develop "a whole black performing technique" that would embody the life style of black people, "the life you find on the street corner, in barber shops, churches and whatever black people do naturally—soul." Black performers don't have to aim at Broadway, because "the Man has reached a dead end creatively, so why should we continue to take our problems to him? He can't even solve his own."

Jessie De Vore, actor-producer of "The Believers," stated in a recent interview that whites can "criticize acting or directing, but if they've never sat for hours on end in a hot, sweaty Deep-South Baptist church on hard, stiff-backed chairs and watched Deacon Miller snoring, they won't know what we're doing on stage. It would be like me trying to evaluate the Talmud."

His words bring to mind again the funeral of Dr. King —the surging crowds before the doors of Ebenezer Baptist Church, trying to get in, despite the fact that there was no room; and inside, exactly the kind of atmosphere De Vore describes: the heaviness and the heat hanging like clouds, the electric emotion as the contralto sang "My Heavenly Father Watches Over Me"; Belafonte struggling with his tears; the glistening perspiration on those stunned distinguished faces—the contrast of life styles. There was something false in the restraint. We knew it. Caught in the terrible electronic cage of television, caught in the instant

commentary, caught in the obvious parallels of the com-
mentators, caught in the clichés and the stereotypes, we
resented the show which the white folks forced upon us;
and when one of the singers burst into tears and covered
her face with the hymnal, we wept too, watching the
screen in our dining room across Fair Street, where the
huge crowds were gathering for the public service on the
Morehouse College campus. That's how we act at funerals,
my wife said. Then King's own voice leapt living from the
tape with all of that majestic power and precision that he
seemed always capable of when occasion demanded: "Say
Martin Luther King, Jr., tried to feed the hungry. Say I
was a drum major for Justice."

Nobody has said it yet, but the time will come when
some fledgling Ph.D. studying the secrets of the King ora-
torical magic will call attention to the grotesqueness of his
imagery and suggest the way it might have been done in
order to complete this pattern or that; and black people will
laugh and black intellectual guerrillas will lash out and say
that long ago Sterling Brown and James Weldon Johnson
called attention to that very type of imagery as characteristic of the black folk tradition; and they will say, White
man, you don't know because you haven't listened to
enough black sermons, and if you started listening when
you were twenty-five, it was too late. You don't have the
Soul-Sounds in your mind.

Remember the *Time* account of the funeral, the pejorative description of the soloist's voice. That "reedy" quality
that the writer disparaged, King loved, because it *is* ours; it
is as old as Africa. It is a black cultural value. It's us. It was
part of Martin Luther King's Soul, the part that doesn't
come through when you read his speeches with a white
American voice, pronouncing all the *r*'s and the *-ing*'s,

squeezing out the history and the proud virtuosity and the pain, squeezing out the Soul with "right angles of the spirit."[13] This is what Mike Thelwell and Vincent Harding are talking about when they attack Styron's presumptuous book. This is why Ossie Davis, the perfect actor to portray *our* Nat Turner, Ossie Davis who delivered the eulogy for Malcolm X, is leading a boycott by black actors directed against the filming of the novel.

Right angles of the spirit! The economics of the slave trade: the most efficient way of packing them in the holds, into the account books, onto the auction blocks. Slash them, bang them, break them—three-quarters of a man, fractioned citizen, percentage integration, *our* negroafroamericanblack Expert, our *data*, our nation of *laws* rather than men, Negro American, *lawandorder*. Plane geometry of death! This is the cage that has always boxed us in.

It boxed in our earliest writers. Phillis Wheatley, that privileged slave, that black prodigy who somehow was unable to come to grips honestly with her blackness, or even the institution of slavery itself, boxed in by the right angles of the heroic couplet, is an early emblem of geometric death. That she was technically skilled is well known and certainly commendable; that the technique was alien and set her apart from her blackness without gaining her admittance to the white pantheon of "American Literature" is another indication of how black people have been manipulated by the white academic and cultural establishment. But even Phillis Wheatley tried to say something about the condition of slavery. In a poem entitled "To the Right Honorable William, Earl of Dartmouth, His Majesty's Principal Secretary of State for North America, etc.," she wrote:

13. This phrase comes from Bennett, *The Negro Mood*, p. 88.

> Should you, my lord, while you pursue my song
> Wonder from whence my love of *Freedom* sprung,
> Whence flow these wishes for the common good,
> By feeling hearts alone best understood,
> I, young in life, by seeming cruel fate
> Was snatch'd from *Afric's* fancy'd happy seat:
> What pangs excruciating must molest,
> What sorrows labour in my parent's breast?
> Steel'd was the soul and by no misery mov'd
> That from a father seiz'd his babe belov'd
> Such, such my case. And can I then but pray
> Others may never feel tyrannic sway?[14]

Others may never feel tyrannic sway! So her awareness is there albeit couched in the circumlocutions of neoclassical diction. But the extent of her estrangement, her assimilation, appears in the words "*Afric's* fancy'd happy seat" and "seeming cruel fate." In her brief poem entitled "On Being Brought from Africa to America" (*Kaleidoscope*, p. 7), we see considerable linguistic evidence of much of the spiritual disease of this country.

> 'Twas mercy brought me from my *Pagan* land,
> Taught my benighted soul to understand
> That there's a God, that there's a *Saviour* too;
> Once I redemption neither sought nor knew.
> Some view our sable race with scornful eye,
> "Their color is a diabolic die."
> Remember, *Christians*, *Negroes*, black as *Cain*,
> May be refined, and join th' angelic train.

Western religion, Western iconography, Western symbol-

---

14. Quoted from *Kaleidoscope: Poems by American Negro Poets*, ed. Robert Hayden (New York: Harcourt, Brace & World, 1967), p. 4.

ism, all conspire to create black self-hatred, black self-denial, black slavery. The permutations of this condition are multitudinous, subtle, and varied, and range from the fossilized fears and hatreds in words like "blackball," "blackmail," and so on, to Shakespeare's Claudius at prayer, saying:

> O wretched state! O bosom black as death!
> O limed soul, that, struggling to be free,
> Art more engag'd! Help, angels! Make assay.
> (Hamlet III. iii. 67–69)

And so Claudius struggles with his blackness, as Cain had struggled with his, the same Cain from whom black men were descended, and the monstrous alien Grendel of *Beowulf*. This equation of blackness and evil forms a strong part of Western attitudes, religious and philosophical as well as social. In the play *Othello*, for example, even Desdemona herself is somewhat ambivalent when she defends her choice of the Moor. Her father's accusation rests on the association of blackness with evil and evil with conjuration, for no one in her right mind would choose so unnatural a mate. Brabantio's speech follows:

> A maiden never bold;
> Of spirit so still and quiet that her motion
> Blush'd at herself; and she—in spite of nature,
> Of years, of country, credit, everything—
> To fall in love with what she fear'd to look on!
> It is a judgment maim'd and most imperfect
> That will confess perfection so could err
> Against all rules of nature, and must be driven
> To find out practices of cunning hell
> Why this should be.   (I. iii. 94–103)

After Othello recounts the manner of his wooing, the fair-minded Duke concedes that "I think this tale would win my daughter too." But when Desdemona speaks in her own behalf there is a certain "liberal" presumptuousness which is quite relevant to this discussion of blackness in America. She says:

> My heart's subdu'd
> Even to the very quality of my lord.
> I saw Othello's visage in his mind,
> And to his honours and his valiant parts
> Did I my soul and fortunes consecrate.
>
> (I. iii. 252–255)

Her words are reminiscent of Phillis Wheatley's admonition:

> Remember, *Christians*, *Negroes*, black as *Cain*,
> May be refined, and join th' angelic train.

Here the word "refined" is important, for it means not only changing one's manner but one's essence almost, like changing petroleum into gasoline. It is no wonder then that many black people have not only rejected Phillis Wheatley but Christianity and Negroes as well, as Black Consciousness seeks the Black Unconscious, the Soul life of the folk. But, finally, in *Othello*, it is the earthy "English" Emilia who makes the typical European association as she confronts Othello:

> *Oth.* She's like a liar gone to burning hell!
> 'Twas I that kill'd her.
>   *Emil.*   O, the more angel she,
> And you the blacker devil!
>
> (v. ii. 129–131)

The devil is black, sin is black, death is black, Cain is black, Grendel is black, Othello is black. Ergo Othello is the devil. The black man is the devil. The devil is the black man! Even a cursory examination of Western iconography reveals the persistence of this conception. Let a single example suffice for the time being, gentle Fra Angelico's "The Last Judgment" in San Marco's in Florence, where the sinners, painted black, are being forced by diabolic underlings into the monstrous black jaws of a black Satan.

One is, of course, aware in all of this of another tradition in the West which, as in Melville, makes whiteness evil. One of my white colleagues mentioned that to me, and I asked him how many people have read Melville—that is, nonacademic people. In fact, how many nonacademic people read novels at all, yet are fundamentally involved in all of the traditional color symbology of the West? Short of a poll, I have no way of documenting an obvious fact—that the pejorative associations which were prevalent in the Middle Ages still affect our thinking today. Not only white people's thinking but black people's as well, and honesty compels me to point out that *our* songs, *our* games, *our* myths embody a good deal of anti-black feeling and attitude. This is the old self-hatred that one hears in the "Dozens" and in the blues. It is, frankly, the *nigger* component of the Black Experience. There is some of it in the lines that I quoted from Phillis Wheatley. There is even more in this blues (traditional lyrics as sung by Wade Newton):

> Go on, black gal, don' try to make me shame'
> Go on, black gal, don' try to make me shame'
> 'Cause your hair is so short I swear to God I can smell
>   your brains.

Or this variation by Lightnin' Hopkins:

> Black gal, O black gal, what make your doggone nappy
> head so hard?
> Black gal, O black gal, what make your doggone nappy
> head so hard?
> Well then, I would come to see you, but your best man
> got me barred.

Or another variation made popular by Louis Jordan and
His Tympany Five during the 1940's.

> Caledonia! Caledonia! What makes your big head so hard?
> MOP!
> Love you, Love you just the same—
> Crazy 'bout you, baby, cause Caledonia is your name.

Caledonia is a black woman: that's why her head is hard.
Black women are evil. Every Negro knows this. Blues and
ballads and slave songs and ditties are full of this self-
hatred. Perhaps the reason we were able to endure it was
that it was so articulated. Perhaps the ironic distance that
literary critics used to talk so much about helped black
people to handle that negative side of their experience, for
in Lightnin' Hopkins' song as well as in "Caledonia" the
love element is still present. In fact, it is the central subject.
Superficially, this says I love you, even though you are
black. Fundamentally, it is a total absorption of the experience of blackness, which in America has been largely
shaped by a reaction to other people's values, to the values
of Europe.

How, then, can you love blackness if your own mind is
messed up? How can you mirror it if the mirror of your

conceptions has been warped by slavery? Notwithstanding, there is a parallel, antithetical almost, tradition of blackness in the folklore. We see it in expressions like, "The blacker the berry, the sweeter the juice." Or in fantastic variations on this quatrain:

> The yellow gal's ridin' on an aeroplane
> The brownskin gal on a train
> The black gal's ridin' on a mule's ass
> But she's ridin' just the same.

And there are variations for men which recall the sharp slave, the Mosca of Ben Jonson, or the slaves in Roman plays, or Anansi the spider of West African folklore—universal types, though for us the roots are all too deep and all too much with us in contemporary colonial America. But to return to the point, not only are these two contradictory attitudes toward one's blackness present at the same time, they are also at times fused. When the fusion is complete, when the contradictions are held together by the force of the poet's passion or imagination we strike the quality of the new poetry, the new Black Consciousness. When the fusion is incomplete, we get the "divided self," the "double self," that DuBois describes and that occupies so large a part of earlier Afro-American writing. At times, a gifted writer like LeRoi Jones or Larry Neal or Eldridge Cleaver gets to a fundamental level which A. B. Spellman calls the Black Unconscious. Here is how it appears in a famous song by Rich Amerson of Alabama.[15]

15. "Black Woman," from "Negro Folk Music of Alabama, Secular" (Ethnic Folkways Library, FE 4417, recorded by Harold Courlander, copyright 1951). The lyrics are adapted from Courlander's transcription; I am indebted to A. B. Spellman for this example, used with permission of Mr. Courlander. Cf. the record for differences in the two transcriptions.

Well, I said come here, Black Woman,
Ah-hmm, don't you hear me cryin', Oh Lordy!
Ah-hmm, I say run here, Black Woman,
I want you to sit on Black Daddy's knee, Lord!
M-hmmm, I know your house feel lonesome,
Ah don't you hear me whoopin', O Lordy!
Don't your house feel lonesome,
When your biscuit-roller gone,
Lord help my cryin' time, don't your house feel lonesome,
Mamma, when your biscuit-roller gone!

I say my house feel lonesome,
I know you hear me cryin' oh Baby!
Ah-hmm, ah, when I looked in my kitchen, Mamma,
And I went all through my dinin' room!
Ah-hmmm, when I woke up this mornin',
I found my biscuit roller done gone!

I'm goin' to Texas, Mamma,
Just to hear the wild ox moan,
Lord help my cryin' time I'm goin' to Texas,
Mamma, to hear the wild ox moan!
And if they moan to suit me,
I'm going to bring a wild ox home!
Ah-hmm, I say I'm got to go to Texas, Black Mamma,
Ah-hmmm, I know I hear me cryin', O Lordy!
Ah-hmmm, I'm got to go to Texas, Black Mamma,
Ah, just to hear the white cow, I say, moan!
Ah-hmmm, ah, if they moan to suit me, Lordy,
I b'lieve I'll bring a white cow back home!

Say, I feel superstitious, Mamma
'Bout my hoggin' bread, Lord help my hungry time,
I feel superstitious, Baby, 'bout my hoggin' bread!
Ah-hmmm, Baby, I feel superstitious,

I say 'stitious, Black Woman!
Ah-hmm, ah you hear me cryin'
About I done got hungry, oh Lordy!
Oh, Mamma, I feel superstitious
About my hog Lord God it's my bread.

I want you to tell me, Mamma,
Ah-hmmm, I hear me cryin', oh Mamma!
Ah-hmmm, I want you to tell me, Black Woman,
Oh where did you stay last night?
I love you, Black Woman,
I tell the whole wide world I do,
Lord help your happy black time, I love you, Baby,
And I tell the world I do!
Ah-hmmm, I love you, Black Woman,
I know you hear me whoopin', Black Baby!
Ah-hmmm, I love you, Black Woman,
And I'll tell your Daddy, I do, Lord!

Remarkable as this is as folk poetry, it is even more so as music when one hears the seventy-year-old Amerson negotiate the falsetto leaps of over an octave on the words "Oh Lordy"; and if one senses the intimate interplay and fusion of the language of love and the language of work, the contrast between the pull of the home and the mysterious wanderlust, then one gets some notion of the vast, virtually untapped power still available to black writers. However, even in this song there is a certain ambiguity of attitude, for example in the "white cow" image because it repeats the imagery of a blues like "Milk Cow," where the cow (though often treated comically) is a profound, primitive metaphor for woman. I say profound and primitive because in this context the male would obviously be the bull, not only the local animals in the singer's mind (with both comic and serious overtones) but the universal symbol of maleness that undergirds so much of world religion and mythology, from the Tassili frescoes to the Masai tribesmen of Kenya, to the ancient gods of Egypt and Babylon, to the bull dancers of Crete, to the god Dionysus and the totem of Mithra, to the bullfights of modern Spain.

This is not too much weight to lay on the poem, since what we are talking about is sex and the mystical exaltation of sex. The bull imagery, like other animal imagery in the blues, shows the awesome primeval power of sex still accessible to the "natchul man." Black people have always known this. Black writers are just beginning to catch up with their musical heritage. In the chapter of Soul on Ice[16] entitled "The Primeval Mitosis," Eldridge Cleaver, though basically known as a political activist, begins to explore this mythic dimension. Larry Neal, Addison Gayle, Jr., W. Kgositsile, Calvin Hernton, A. B. Spellman, to name a few of the younger writers—all approach it in varying ways, for they know the awesome power there waiting for the poet's ju-ju.

But the hangups of American life make it difficult at times to get back to the Black Unconscious. The condition of the black bourgeoisie is well known through Franklin Frazier's work of that name and through Nathan Hare's The Black Anglo-Saxons and through other studies of varying importance and accuracy. Frank Marshall Davis has a series of humorous poems on the ambiguities of this class. The following (quoted from Kaleidoscope, p. 5) is typical:

16. New York: McGraw-Hill, 1968.

Robert Whitmore

Having attained success in business
possessing three cars
one wife and two mistresses
a home and furniture
talked of by the town
and thrice ruler of the local Elks
Robert Whitmore
died of apoplexy
when a stranger from Georgia
mistook him
for a former Macon waiter.

Mari Evans, in "Black Jam for Dr. Negro,"[17] expresses the
hangups as sexual challenge.

Pullin me in off the corner to wash my face an
cut my afro turn
my collar
down
when that aint my
thang I
walk heels first
nose round an tilted
up
my ancient
eyes
see your thang
baby
and it aint
shit

17. See *Black Voices: An Anthology of Negro Literature*, ed.
Abraham Chapman (New York: New American Library, 1968),
pp. 481–482.

your thang
puts my eyes out baby
turns my seeking fingers
    into splintering fists
messes up my head
an I scream you out
your thang
is whats wrong
    an you keep
    pilin it on rubbin it
    in
    smoothly
    doin it
    to death

what you sweatin
baby

                your guts
puked an rotten
waitin
to be defended

Before the black bourgeoisie can save itself, before Negroes can become black people, they have to confront their
blackness and repudiate all that makes them ashamed of it.
This is the important step on the road to self-knowledge
and self-regeneration which the nameless hero of *Invisible
Man*[18] has to take. The novel is as vital now as it was when
it was first published. The main difference, however, is that
black self-consciousness has traveled since that time from

18. The following quotations from Ralph Ellison's *Invisible Man*
are from the Signet Edition (New York: New American Library,
1952).

self-knowledge to self-determination.[19] In the following
passage, the hero has suffered the trauma of the Niggerzone, the loss of black identity which results from self-
repudiation and the absorption of the white values symbol-
ized by his college education in the South and his trust in
President Bledsoe and the whole white power structure
that he represents. The soulless efficiency of urban in-
dustrial life has conspired with Southern education to rob
him of his identity. He goes "home" to Harlem, and as he
passes the "endless succession" of shops, blinking his eyes in
the wintry air, he is drawn to a window "decorated with
switches of wiry false hair, ointments guaranteed to produce the miracle of whitening black skin. 'You too can be
truly beautiful,' a sign proclaimed. 'Win happiness with
whiter complexion. Be outstanding in your social set.' " He
quickly walks by, "suppressing a savage urge to push my
fist through the pane" (p. 228). As the hero tries to get
himself together, his mind confused, wondering where he is
going to find a place to sleep, he spies an old black man
warming himself by "an odd-looking wagon, from which a
stovepipe reeled off a thin spiral of smoke that drifted the
odor of baking yams slowly to me, bringing a stab of swift
nostalgia."

"How much are your yams?" I said, suddenly hungry.

"They ten cents and they sweet," he said, his voice quavering
with age. "These ain't none of them binding ones neither. These
here is real, sweet, yaller yams. How many?"

19. One is, of course, aware of the Garvey Movement and its
practical steps. The significance of the present nationalist trend
is its broad range—all the way from control of local schools to
identification with the politics of Africa and the "Third World."
Hence the need for reading the practical writings of the activists
who are not primarily concerned with writing as such.

"One," I said. "If they're that good, one should be enough."

He gave me a searching glance. There was a tear in the corner of his eye. (pp. 228–229)

The old man opens the improvised oven and takes out the yam and starts to put it in a bag.

"Never mind the bag, I'm going to eat it. Here . . ."

"Thanks." He took the dime. "If that ain't a sweet one, I'll give you another one free of charge."

I knew that it was sweet before I broke it; bubbles of brown syrup had burst the skin.

"Go ahead and break it," the old man said. "Break it and I'll give you some butter since you goin' eat it right here. Lots of folks takes 'em home. They got their own butter at home." (p. 229)

The old man in a simple but profound gesture of love pours a spoonful of butter over the yam. And when the hero eats this ceremonial meal he is momentarily reunited with his people, though not quite so free, as we discover later, of the system of which Bledsoe is a part. But he renounces Bledsoe.

I took a bite, finding it as sweet and hot as any I'd ever had, and was overcome with such a surge of homesickness that I turned away to keep my control. I walked along, munching the yam, just as suddenly overcome by an intense feeling of freedom—simply because I was eating while walking along the street. It was exhilarating. I no longer had to worry about who saw me or about what was proper. To hell with all that, and as sweet as the yam actually was, it became like nectar with the thought. If only someone who had known me at school or at home would come along and see me now. How shocked they'd be! I'd push them into a side street and smear their

faces with the peel. What a group of people we were, I thought.
Why, you could cause us the greatest humiliation simply by
confronting us with something we liked. Not *all* of us, but so
many. Simply by walking up and shaking a set of chitterlings
or a well-boiled hog maw at them during the clear light of day!
What consternation it would cause! (pp. 229–230)

In the ecstasy of his reverie, he imagines himself confronting Bledsoe (Dr. Thomas, Dr. Negro) in the "crowded
lobby of Men's House." Bledsoe sees him, but tries to cool
it. The hero becomes enraged and "whipping out a foot or
two of chitterlings, raw, uncleaned and dripping sticky
circles on the floor," shakes them in Bledsoe's face, shout-
ing:

> "Bledsoe, you're a shameless chitterling eater! I accuse you
> of relishing hog bowels! Ha! And not only do you eat them,
> you sneak and eat them in *private* when you think you're
> unobserved! You're a sneaking chitterling lover! I accuse you
> of indulging in a filthy habit, Bledsoe! Lug them out of there,
> Bledsoe! Lug them out so we can see! I accuse you before
> the eyes of the world!" And he lugs them out, yards of them,
> with mustard greens, and racks of pigs' ears, and pork chops
> and black-eyed peas with dull accusing eyes. (p. 230)

This accusation would be worse than accusing him of rap-
ing "an old woman of ninety-nine years, weighing ninety
pounds . . . blind in one eye and lame in the hip." Bledsoe
would drop his head in shame, and lose caste. And all of the
weekly newspapers would attack him with this caption
over his picture: *Prominent Educator Reverts to Field Nig-
gerism.* They would demand that "either he recant or retire
from public life." He would lose the support of his good
white folks, and he would end up "an exile washing dishes

at the Automat. For down South he would be unable to get a job on the honey wagon" (p. 231).

But this white-mindedness also pervades the other classes. Richard Wright was quite aware of this, too, and in the essay "How 'Bigger' Was Born," he lists five black proto-types of his character: the bully, the beat, the "bad nigger," the manic-depressive, and the black rebel. There were many, subtle variations of these types, in a spectrum which Wright explains this way:

. . . because the blacks were so *close* to the very civilization which sought to keep them out, because they could not *help* but react in some way to its incentives and prizes, and because the very tissue of their consciousness received its tone and timbre from the strivings of that dominant civilization, oppression spawned among them a myriad variety of reactions, reaching from outright blind rebellion to a sweet, otherworldly submissiveness. (*Black Voices*, p. 543)

This spectrum still persists; and the wigs and the skin whiteners that the hero of Ellison's *Invisible Man* saw in the store windows can still be seen in any black community today, can still be seen in our newspaper ads and in our magazines. The black community in Atlanta is representative. Walk down Auburn Avenue or West Hunter Street and the number of wig shops will amaze you. They do a thriving business off the old values (and, one might add, a perversion of the new ones, too). Processed hair is still in. That is why we hear the black voice of Le Graham cross-cutting the "konk-haired hipsters," rip-sawing the "wig-wearing whores," and behind it we hear Malcolm X Shabazz and Elijah Muhammad, and behind them the Seventh Day Adventists and the voices of the Holiness churches, and behind them still, in the Niggerzone of the Dozens and the Blues, the voice of Jimmie Rushing, "Mr. Five by Five," rapping on his woman:

I did more for you, baby, than the Good Lord ever done.
I did more for you, ba-a-by, than the Good Lord ever done:
I even bought you some hair when the Good Lord didn't give you none.

Black writers, black poets, black artists are trying to demolish that self-hatred, and their efforts are beginning to have effect. The Blackstone Rangers of Chicago have gone "natural" to improve their image (How could they not be affected by the Wall of Respect?); and James Brown's fans pressured him into doing the same; and for the women the example of Abbie Lincoln and Miriam Makeba has been very persuasive. Other Soul Sisters and Brothers are still "going through changes." Aretha Franklin is reportedly under pressure to give up her elaborate collection of wigs. Diana Ross and Dionne Warwick have worn Afro wigs during public performances; and Leslie Uggams has incurred the wrath of many black women for many reasons but most recently for her backing of a firm that makes Afro wigs—out of nylon.[20]

This preoccupation with hair is emblematic of the black man's estrangement from himself, from his own ideal of the "natchul man." Although some of the brothers and sisters are involved in a kind of fad and, natural-haired or no, have "processed minds," in Rap Brown's words, the gesture of going natural has about it a commitment to a new vision of oneself, as a black man or woman, not as a Negro. It is a

20. See *Jet*, Oct. 31, 1968, p. 37. Apparently many of these kinds of wigs are also being bought by whites, which, to use Julius Lester's expression, is "a thing unto itself."

declaration of independence. At times the change obviously triggers some hidden strength. When lovely Mari Evans, for example, "went natural," it seemed to coincide with a powerful burst of creative energy; and a comparison of her recent poetry with the skilful but stylized earlier performances seems to bear this out. Like the hero of Ellison's novel, she, to use her own words, became "beautifully and incontrovertibly black." Certainly no white person can fully understand this phenomenon—one even doubts whether Africans can understand it this way unless they have lived in this country, since they largely haven't suffered the special kind of personal and ethnic deracination that Afro-Americans have endured. (Black South Africans are probably an exception.)

A generation ago, another beautiful black woman, Margaret Walker, focused all of that world of meaning that I have been trying to suggest in "For My People," probably the most comprehensively Soulful poem ever written. She tells it "like it is." Here is a section of that poem:

> For my playmates in the clay and dust and sand of Alabama backyards playing baptizing and preaching, and doctor and jail and soldier and school and mama and cooking and playhouse and concert and store and Miss Choomby and hair and company;
> For the cramped bewildered years we went to school to learn to know the reasons why and the answers to and the people who and the places where and the days when, in memory of the bitter hours when we discovered we were black and poor and small and different and nobody wondered and nobody understood;

> (*American Negro Poetry*, pp. 128–129)

Only a black American, I submit, can fully understand all
of the tremendous emotional weight which that single
word "hair" receives in this poem. It is almost as though the
whole experience of blackness were there.

Thus it is impossible to understand the revolutionary
black literature without understanding the people to whom
it is addressed, without understanding some of the earlier
writers, as I have implied, as well as those presently engaged. For in this writing black people are not only the
poets and the audience, they are also the poems. This is
implicit in the poetry of Langston Hughes, and, in a subtle
sense in the character of Simple, developed over many
years in his prose sketches. It is implicit in the life of
Langston Hughes. It is implicit in the poetry of Margaret
Walker and Gwendolyn Brooks. It is implicit in the cultural heroes of black people: Malcolm X, LeRoi Jones,
Muhammad Ali, Charlie Parker, John Coltrane, Thelonius
Monk, Martin Luther King, W. E. B. DuBois, Frederick
Douglass. The list may change from poet to poet, but the
poet knows that the people know, that it is the people who
judge. Here is Le Graham again (see p. 77, above):

Black poems are beautiful
egyptian princesses. afro-americans. john o. killens. ossie
                              davis. leroi jones. mal
                              colm x shabazz. robert
                              williams. lumumba. A
poem for wooly-haired brothers. natural-haired sisters.
Bimbos. boots & woogies. Or nappy-headed youngsters
                              Cause they want what i
                              want: . . .

Don L. Lee puts it this way: "Black poets will live their
poems; they, themselves, will be poems" (see n. 9, above).

Langston Hughes was our most comprehensive embodiment of this sentiment, and his recent death occasioned an outpouring of poetry which was occasionally on the level of black genius, that is to say, Soul. He was, thus, not only the Poem, he was the living source of his own resurrection in others. In April of this year, that tragic month, we lost one of our finest young writers, Conrad Kent Rivers, who had written thus of Langston Hughes, in a poem entitled "For All Things Black and Beautiful."

For all things black and beautiful,
The brown faces you loved so well and long,
The endless roads leading back to Harlem.
   For all things black and beautiful
   The seeking and the labor always waiting and coming
   Until you began to dream of Nubian queens
   And black kings shifting the dust of eternity
   Before the white man brought his shame and God.
   For all things black and beautiful
   It took a lot of stones from little white boys
   To produce the poem and quench the first desire to taste
   Their nectar and the black wine of black empires
   Flowing through your black bursting body.

. . . .

For all things black and beautiful
The music you heard in the hallways and hid in the noun
The street woman you loved and saved with a sober ballad
The urban holocaust that swept you through the ghetto-ghetto
   land
The barbecue and sweet potatoes too many nights you went
   without
The sounds you heard in your head like dripping meal from
   cornbread

The Renaissance and Du Bois and Roberson and Carl and Arna
and Zora
All gone like a Russian moon passes through the bight of Benin.
For all things black and beautiful
And Mali rising again and Timbuctu spreading culture across
the land
And Yardbird smoking and cleansing this roomy world of dry
ashes
Until Sweet Sue understands the beauty of her black sunset
silk skin
And the glory of her carmelite brown brighter than a blue red
sun
Echoing the ancient truths of her own black culture and being.
For all things black and beautiful seen through your eyes:
Willie Mays doing his ballet in centerfield and Lady Day pray-
ing
And Harlem The Black Mother weeping and my own wet
eyes, Langston
Feeling the darkness and the decline of the kingdom and glory
of all
Things you made so black and beautiful in your fashion and
way.
Africa is in your grave and may all the elements find peace
with you.

(Negro Digest, Sept. 1967, pp. 32, 34)

And Larry Neal in a magnificent poem, "Don't Say Goodbye to the Pork-Pie Hat," saw in Hughes the embodiment
of the jazz experience. The legendary pork-pie hat was
worn by both Hughes and Lester Young, The Prez, genius
of the alto saxophone.

> Don't say goodbye to the pork-pie hat that rolled
> along on padded shoulders,

>   that swang be-bop phrases
>   in Minton's jelly-roll dreams.
> don't say goodbye to hip hats tilted in the style of
>   a soulful era,
> the pork-pie hat that Lester dug,
> swirling in the sound of sun saxes,
> repeating phrase on phrase, repeating bluely
> as hi-hat cymbals crash and trumpets scream while
> musicians move in and out of this gloom; the
>   pork-pie hat reigns supreme,
> the elegance of style
> gleaned from the city's underbelly.
>   tonal memories
>   tonal memories
> of salt-peanuts and hot house birds. the pork-pie hat
>   sees.
>   (*Negro Digest*, Sept. 1967, p. 46)

In the specifics of the life of Lester Young, the poet adumbrates the texture of the Poem which is Langston Hughes, which is black people, which is Soul.

> Sounds drift above the cities of Black America;
> all over America black musicians are putting
> on the pork-pie hat again, picking up their axes,
> preparing to blow away the white dream. you can
> hear them screeching love in rolling sheets of sound;
> with movement and rhythm recreating themselves and the
>   world;
> sounds splintering the deepest regions of the spiritual
>   universe—
> crisp and moaning voices leaping in the horns of destruc-
>   tion,

blowing doom and death to all who have no use for the
   Spirit.
don't say goodbye to the pork-pie hat, it lives. Yeah . . .
                        (*Negro Digest*, Sept. 1967, p. 48)

This identification of the poet and the musician is natural.
Our profoundest poets are musicians or dancers. Our profoundest preachers are poets. Bluesman Son House shouts,
"I'm gonna preach these blues." And Son House, a former
preacher, is a poet. Accordingly, in "Two Jazz Poems,"
young Carl Hines describes an ancient black musician as he
lifts the saxophone to his mouth.

> gently he lifts it now
> to parted lips. see? to
> tell all the world that
> he is a Black Man. that
> he was sent here to preach
> the Black Gospel of Jazz.
>
>   (*American Negro Poetry*, p. 186)

A generation earlier, the young Langston Hughes wrote:

> Oh, silver tree!
> Oh, shining rivers of the soul.
>
> In a Harlem cabaret
> Six long-headed jazzers play.
> A dancing girl whose eyes are bold
> Lifts high a dress of silken gold.
>
>   (*American Negro Poetry*, p. 63)

He knew and understood the profound source of the jazz
impulse, and he never ceased to pursue it in his own poetry.
Long before the beat poets, he read his poetry to jazz
combos. He knew that black life in America has found its

most ancient and meaningful expression in music and dance and the poetry of the spoken word. Sterling Brown knew this too, and James Weldon Johnson, so that Johnson would, in a hymn of his own, address the "Black and Unknown Bards" who created our earliest music:

> There is a wide, wide wonder in it all,
> That from degraded rest and servile toil
> The fiery spirit of the seer should call
> These simple children of the sun and soil.
> O black slave singers, gone, forgot, unfamed,
> You—you alone, of all the long, long line
> Of those who've sung untaught, unknown, unnamed,
> Have stretched out upward, seeking the divine.
>
> *(American Negro Poetry*, p. 1)

Johnson was fascinated by the oral poetry of the black country preacher whose vision and power he suggested in a volume of poems entitled, aptly enough, *God's Trombones.* And just as Conrad Rivers sees through Langston's eyes "Willie Mays doing his ballet in centerfield and Lady Day praying"—the blues—so Sterling Brown would thank Jack Johnson for his manly courage, his "golden, spacious grin," and would recall Ma Rainey, like some ancient black priestess purging her people's hearts of sorrow.[21]

> O Ma Rainey,
> Sing yo' song;
> Now you's back
> Whah you belong,
> Git way inside us,

21. See *Southern Road* (New York: Harcourt, Brace, 1932); the reference to Jack Johnson is from "Strange Legacies," p. 95; the "Ma Rainey" verses are from pp. 63–64.

> Keep us strong. . . .
> O Ma Rainey,
> Li'l an' low;
> Sing us 'bout de hard luck
> Roun' our do';
> Sing us 'bout de lonesome road
> We mus' go. . . .

I talked to a fellow, an' the fellow say,
"She jes' catch hold of us, somekindaway.
She sang Backwater Blues one day:

> *'It rained fo' days an' de skies was dark as night,*
> *Trouble taken place in de lowlands at night.*
>
> *'Thundered an' lightened an' the storm began to roll*
> *Thousan's of people ain't got no place to go.*
>
> *'Den I went an' stood upon some high ol' lonesome hill,*
> *An' looked down on the place where I used to live.'*

An' den de folks, dey natchally bowed dey heads an' cried,
Bowed dey heavy heavy heads, shet dey moufs up tight an'
    cried,
An' Ma lef' de stage, an' followed some de folks outside."

Dere wasn't much more de fellow say:
She jes' gits hold of us dataway.

More recently, Charlie Parker and John Coltrane have
exerted a gigantic influence upon the development of music
in the United States. They, too, have got hold of us, have
got "way inside us," and set dazzling with blackness the
minds of those who hear them still as they screech "love in
rolling sheets of sound." Parker was blackness, Coltrane
was blackness—the full spectrum of it, grounded at both
ends in spirit. A. B. Spellman is one of the finest interpreters
of the development of this music, both in his criticism and

in his poetry. He asks in the more recent of two poems on Coltrane: "did john's music kill him?"[22]

in the morning part
of evening he would stand
before his crowd. the voice
would call his name &
redlight fell around him.
jimmy'd bow a quarter hour
til mccoy fed block chords
to his stroke. elvin's thunder
roll & eric's scream. then john.

then john. *little old lady*
had a nasty mouth. *summertime*
when the war is. *africa* ululating
a line bunched up like itself
into knots paints beauty black.

trane's horn had words in it
i know when i sleep sober & dream
those dreams i duck in the world
of sun & shadow. yet even in the day john
& a little grass put them on me clear
as tomorrow in a glass enclosure.

kill me john my life eats
life. the thing that beats out of
me happens in a vat enclosed
& fermenting & wanting to explode
like your song.

      so beat john's death words down
      on me in the darker part
      of evening. the black light issued
      from him in the pit he made

22. Unpublished; quoted with permission of the author.

> around us. worms came clear
> to me where i thought i had been
> brilliant. o john death will
> not contain you death
> will not contain you

What Coltrane signifies for black people because of the
breadth of his vision and the incredible energy behind his
spiritual quest, Malcolm X signifies in another way—not as
musician, but simply and profoundly as black man, as Black
Experience, and that experience in process of discovering
itself, of celebrating itself. Although his assassination and
funeral did not occasion the national paroxysms of guilt
and gloating hatred in the white community that Dr.
King's death did, in a way it affected black writers and
black intellectuals much more deeply. For there always
was, tacitly understood, something curiously unreal and,
upon reflection, wonderfully naive about the optimistic
philosophy of nonviolence which made one feel somehow
protective toward Dr. King. There was also something in
the personality and background of the man—the mere fact
that he was a preacher and a formally educated man (Dr.
King)—which, while no obstacle to the loving, suffering
black multitudes of the South, made it difficult for the
Northern, urban, hip young blacks to identify with him.
The abstractions of brotherhood and universal love were
difficult to believe in after a day with the Man, or after a
night with the blues.

Chicago signaled the dimensions of the urban alienation.
In addition to a powerful political machine, theology stood
in the way. Nonviolence was not natural. Self-defense was.
And when we remember the terrible anguish that King
endured as he tried to come to grips with the power of

Black Power, we realize that there was some limitation in
his early life which precluded his solving the problem in
time. That limitation was insufficient knowledge of black
ghetto life. Of course, he knew the poverty, and he deliberately subjected himself to it; and he knew immense suffering and anguish. Of course, he sympathized with and loved
the poor people, the common people; he was like Langston
Hughes in this, and he never tired of quoting the poet's
"Mother to a Son," with the line, "Life for me ain' been no
crystal stair." And it hadn't been, with his beautiful mind
and his raw courage and his pride. But he didn't know the
pimps and the whores and the dope pushers that the black
poets both love and hate and try to change—the "konk-
haired hipsters. wig-wearing whores."

Malcolm X Shabazz knew them. He had been a konk-
haired hipster and he had been a pimp and he had been a
hustler and a dope addict. But he went through changes.
Rough changes! And paid more dues than any man on
record. And he was baptized into blackness and repudiated
his slave name (Little.—How inappropriate it was!) and
became Malcolm X—indicating the lost part of his life and
history. He went through more changes—beautiful
changes—and became, after his pilgrimage to Mecca, El-
Hajj Malik El-Shabazz. In some ways, his death was more
tragic than King's, for the Movement had moved North
and he had the potential of unifying elements in the black
community that King could not reach. Moreover, his life,
though full, was less complete than King's. Though King's
death was every bit as brutal, there was a tragic beauty in
the logic of it and in King's almost mystical intuition of it.[23]

23. Cf. Malcolm's own logical, practical, political awareness
that he was a "doomed" man, in *The Autobiography of Malcolm
X.*

King the prophet had steadily seen the Promised Land;
Malcolm the prophet had just discerned the way. It would
have been inevitable that they would have met later to
work for the good of their people—together. There is small
reason why one should not suspect treachery and conspir-
acy. There is every justification for LeRoi Jones's rage in
"Poem for Black Hearts," from the collection, *For Malcolm X*.[24]

> For Malcolm's eyes, when they broke
> the face of some dumb white man. For
> Malcolm's hands raised to bless us
> all black and strong in his image
> of ourselves, for Malcolm's words
> fire darts, the victor's tireless
> thrusts, words hung above the world
> change as it may, he said it, and
> for this he was killed, for saying,
> and feeling, and being/change, all
> collected hot in his heart, For Malcolm's
> pleas for your dignity, black men, for your life,
> black men, for the filling of your minds
> with righteousness, For all of him dead and
> gone and vanished from us, and all of him which
> clings to our speech black god of our time.
> For all of him, and all of yourself, look up,
> black man, quit stuttering and shuffling, look up,
> black man, quit whining and stooping, for all
>   of him,
> For Great Malcolm a prince of the earth, let
>   nothing in us rest

24. Ed. Dudley Randall and Margaret G. Burroughs (Detroit:
Broadside Press, 1967), pp. 61–62.

until we avenge ourselves for his death, stupid
  animals
that killed him, let us never breathe a pure
  breath if
we fail, and white men call us faggots till the
  end of
the earth.

But equally there is justification for our hope, for his gift
was Black Manhood. Edward S. Spriggs, in "For Brother
Malcolm," wrote:

> there is no memorial site
> in harlem
> save the one we are building
> in the street of
> our young minds
> till our hands & eyes
> have strength to mould
> the concrete beneath our feet
>
> (*For Malcolm* X, p. 73)

And in Gwendolyn Brooks's poem, "Malcolm X," we see
the resolution of the identity problem, for Malcolm's manhood recreates us all, in self-knowledge and in love.

Original.
Hence ragged-round,
Hence rich-robust.

He had the hawk-man's eyes.
We gasped. We saw the maleness.
The maleness raking out and making guttural the air
And pushing us to walls.

And in a soft and fundamental hour
A sorcery devout and vertical
Beguiled the world.

He opened us—
Who was a key.

Who was a man.

(*For Malcolm* X, p. 3)

Julius Lester, columnist for *The National Guardian* and
an editor of *Sing Out,* is a versatile and talented young
man. He is both tough and sensitive. He has absorbed the
blues tradition as singer and composer, and has extended it
in his own songs. He loves his people; he is his people. He
has attacked their enemies. He has suffered for them, and
he has recorded their beauty in hundreds of masterful photographs that he took as a field secretary for SNCC. He
signs his letters "Love and Revolution." He writes sparse
evocative poetry, but his most beautiful poem he saved for
his son. He baptized him in blackness. He named him
Malcolm Coltrane!

Lest we forget, let us repeat again the names of Langston Hughes and Sterling Brown, black grandfathers of the
new poetry, for both realized in their poetry the distinctive
life style of their people. Let us recall that in 1939 Saunders
Redding, in *To Make a Poet Black* (University of North
Carolina Press), described the work of Hughes in this
manner.

Hughes is the most prolific and the most representative
of the new Negroes. By training and experience he is at the
opposite end from Cullen, that is to say, he is a Negro divinely
capable of realizing (which is instinctive) and giving expression to (which is cultivated) the dark perturbation of
the soul—there is no other word—of the Negro. There is

this difference between racial thought and feelings: what the professors, the ministers, the physicians, the social workers think, the domestics, the porters, the dock hands, the factory girls, and the streetwalkers feel—in a great tide that pours over into song and shout, prayer and cursing, laughter and tears. More than any other writer of the race, Langston Hughes has been swept with this tide of feeling. This accounts for the fresh green of him, the great variety of his moods. (p. 115)

Notice how Redding has used the word "soul," almost completely with its present connotations. This is important historically, for it indicates a precise awareness of our life style about the time the term "negritude" was coined and, certainly, long before the current usage of the term "Soul." Perhaps at this point one should elaborate the concept a little and suggest its importance to the contemporary black writer and to the present black community. The best description that I know of appears in the words of Lerone Bennett, in *The Negro Mood:*

The whole corpus of the tradition . . . is compressed into the folk myth of *Soul,* the American counterpart of the African *Negritude,* a distinct quality of Negro-ness growing out of the Negro's experience and not his genes. *Soul* is a metaphorical evocation of Negro being as expressed in the Negro tradition. It is the feeling with which an artist invests his creation, the style with which a man lives his life. It is, above all, the spirit rather than the letter: a certain way of feeling, a certain way of expressing oneself, a certain way of being. (p. 89)

Bennett further describes Soul as "a relaxed and noncompetitive approach to being, a complex acceptance of the contradictions of life, a buoyant sadness, a passionate spontaneity, and a gay sorrow." This tradition of Soul is "very definitely nonmachine, but it is not antimachine; it simply recognizes that machines are generative power and not soul, instruments and not ends. It is this insight which draws us to the Harlems of the mind" (p. 89). Bennett calls Soul the American counterpart to negritude. Others make no distinction between the two concepts; while difficult to describe, they do exist and should be pointed out.

In the first place, it should be stressed that Soul is not a theory or an intuition which has grown out of the nostalgia of a group of expatriate black intellectuals but a highly condensed potent folk myth which black Americans are exploring and living every day. President Senghor's unlettered countrymen doubtless would not even use the term "negritude" when talking about themselves or among themselves, even though the substance of their lives and conversation may well be subsumed under that term. With "Soul," however, it is different. Not only do the unlettered use it, but the Ph.D. as well. Not only adults, but children. Although there is a good deal of variation in the way that individuals express it, there is common consent as to its deep intuitive, ethnic meaning. It has the historical specificity of our black lives here: a certain kind of walk ("Ooh-ba-ditty, you walk so pretty" or "walk that walk"), a certain kind of talk, of gesture and dance, of attitude.

The parallels with negritude are thus fairly obvious. Among them are the emphasis on intuition, the dance, the power of the Word, wholeness, harmony. Among the obvious differences, however, are the common suffering resulting from the slave experience;[25] the specific popular music that is derived from gospel and blues; the "bad nig-

25. Although this is paralleled in the colonial experience, the deracination and loss of historical continuity set the black Americans apart.

ger" syndrome; the concept of hipness; the celebration of virtuosity; the reconciliation of antipathies, and so on. Gospel chord progressions are specifically Afro-American, but the melismatic style, in this case, African; the improvisation is both African and Afro-American; the powerfully dramatic and lyrical singing, the fluid body rhythms belong to both worlds. But again, "Soul food" not only moves ceremonially in the direction of the slave experience but historically in the direction of Africa, as in the case of the hero in Ellison's novel as he breaks open the hot sweet yam and eats it on the Harlem street.[26] Again, Soul food and Soul cooking incorporate culinary habits preserved from Africa. This is especially true of certain dishes that, while not commonly called "Soul food," certainly are "down-home food," the earlier ethnic designation (at a time when "Down-Home," not Africa, was a kind of Old Country for the transplanted blacks who had gone North for a better life). Such kinds of foods are the red beans and rice of Louisiana and the gumbo of that state, the okra soup of Florida, and the pepper-pots of those regions. It is as though we were dealing with two levels of ethnic memory, one of them recovered through intuition and scholarship, and closer in time and space—the urban memory of a rural past in the New World, an unconscious embodiment of the survival of Africa as tone, feeling, perception, style.

One of the fascinating things about the new black writing is the presence of men like William K. Kgositsile, of South Africa, and Lebert Bethune, of Jamaica, who absorbed the Afro-American Soul into their own African and West Indian consciousness respectively, much in the manner of Claude McKay, of the Harlem Renaissance, a gener-

26. Dr. King was talking about "soul food" and the original "soul music" just a few minutes before he died.

ation ago; and the consciousness of blackness is thus further refined and enlarged, not by scholarship, but by intuition.

Kgositsile's vision is a Pan-Africanism that includes all Africans everywhere. Slender, frail, about five feet tall, he is nonetheless a dynamo of energy and moral sensibility. He speaks thunders in his poems or sings with liquid fire. He is an eloquent spokesman for the new poets, and his own poetry suggests the beginning of a new synthesis of modern African and Afro-American literature. In his poetic credo, "The Impulse Is Personal," he strikes the tone of his black American brothers.

There is nothing like art—in the oppressor's sense of art. There is only movement. Force. Creative power. The walk of the Sophiatown tsotsi or my Harlem brother on Lenox Avenue. Field hollers. The Blues. A Trane riff. Marvin Gaye or mbaqanga. Anguished happiness. Creative power, in whatever form it is released, moves like the dancer's muscles.

But the impulse is personal. (*Negro Digest*, July 1968, p. 42)

Willy speaks from Black Africa to Black America; from Black America to Black Africa. He is of both worlds but not divided. There is a powerful harmony within him, a universal blackness. In "The Elegance of Memory" section of "Point of Departure: Fire Dance Fire Song," he writes:

> There are memories between us
> Deeper than grief. There are
> Feelings between us much stronger
> Than the cold enemy machine that breaks
> The back. Sister, there are places between us
> Deeper than the ocean, no distances.
> Pry your heart open, Brother, mine too,

Learn to love the clear voice
The music in the memory pried
Open to the bone of feeling, no distances
                    (*Negro Digest*, July 1968, p. 45)

In the "Fire Dance" section of the poem, we hear his
thunders:

There will be no dreaming of escape
There will be no bullshit coldwar talk
    The fire burns to re-create
    the rhythms of our timeless acts
    This fire burns timeless in our
    time to destroy all nigger chains
    as real men and women emerge
    from the ruins of the rape by white greed
                    The rape by
    Savages without soul. Savages who want control
    of us, memory, nature. Savages who even forge
    measures to try to control time. Don't you
    know time is not a succession of hours!
    Time is always NOW, don't you know!
    Listen to the drums. That there is a point of
      departure
    NOW is always the time. Praise be to Charlie
      Parker
Now sing a song NOW
A song of the union of pastandfuture
Sing a song of blood. . . .
                    (*Negro Digest*, July 1968, p. 47)

Although Lebert Bethune was born in Jamaica and grew
up there, he has lived much of his adult life in Europe and
the United States. Africa is in his blood, but so is Harlem.

He, too, is Soul, as we see in his "Apollo at the Apollo: 125th St. Harlem."[27]

> With his deep frightless eyes
> His white deltoids
> His pure marble fig-leaf
> That frozen pose for the camera
> His hairless plotted thighs—Apollo
> Could never recognize himself
> Or
> At the heart of the gushing laughter
> Dare to risk a word about his real connections
> No
> Here with Screaming Jay Hawkins and
> The Wild Man from Borneo
> The Raylettes
> Martha and the Vandellas
> Not to mention those two hot Mommas
> Lil and Ella Mae—one black one yellow—
> Who waggle between acts
> Like real live jelly jelly from the roll
> That kinda god
> Would have to trade his fig for meat
> That kinda god would have to trade his pose for motion
> That kinda god
> Would have to lose his timelessness
> "TONIGHT! LIVE! at the APOLLO"

The black vitality which Bethune opposes to the classical Western god, he, like his American brothers, celebrates in the black manhood of Malcolm X. He, like Kgositsile, speaks to Africans everywhere as he fashions in his poetry

27. From *Juju of My Own* (Paris: Des Presses de l'Imprimerie Union à Paris, 1965), p. 13.

and his films and his plays "a Juju of my own." He knows that in every black man's ear there is the voice of the ancient grandmother singing as she bakes "the pliant red clay,"

> "Me no care for Bakra whip
> Me no care fe fum-fum
> Come Juju come"
>
> (*Juju of My Own*, p. 11)

A young Fisk University poet, Donald Graham, expresses Soul this way:

> coltrane must understand how
>   I feel when i hear
> some un-sunned-be-bop jazz-man
>   try
>
> to find the cause of a man's hurt
>
> soul ain't nice it's daddy's backache
>   the blues my mother felt when she
>   bore me
>   in a rat-infested-harlem u.s.a.
>
>   its . . .
>   mammas love and daddys hate—
>   doing it my way
>   survival motion set to music[28]

This is a very beautiful poem and highly significant for the purpose of this discussion. However, I won't finger it with analysis, but simply point out the proprietary assumption behind it. Soul is a black man's thing. Coltrane is a black demigod who suffered himself into the music that the white

28. From *Black Song* (New York: Elam Press, 1966), p. [8].

professional tries to play. Soul ain't nice. It's "survival motion set to music." And what is survival motion? If you're
black, you don't have to ask. If you're not then you must
know that it's not only the "Boogaloo" or the "Tighten
Up," it's also the black worker in the field seen through the
vistas of four hundred years. It's the railroad man linin'
track:

> A nickle's worth of bacon and a dime's worth of lard,
> I would buy more but the time's too hard. . . .

And:

> Capn' got a pistol and he try to play bad,
> But I'm gonna take it if he makes me mad. . . .[29]

It's the motion of the convict's hammer:

> Burner tore his—hunh—
> Black heart away.
> Burner tore his—hunh—
> Black heart away.
> Got me life, bebby,
> An' a day.[30]

It's the movement of Mari Evens' poem, "Vive Noir!"[31]

> i
> am going to rise
> en masse

29. *The Book of Negro Folklore*, ed. Langston Hughes and
Arna Bontemps (New York: Dodd, Mead, 1958), p. 401.

30. Sterling Brown, "Southern Road," quoted from *Book of
Negro Folklore*, p. 547 (originally published in *Southern Road*).

31. *Negro Digest*, Sept./Oct. 1968, pp. 82–84. The two lines
referring to "Coppertone" that appear in this publication are
omitted, following a conversation with the poet in May 1968. The
omission strengthens the poem. Reprinted by permission of the
poet.

        from Inner City
                        sick
                of newyork ghettos
                chicago tenements
            l a's slums

Then she details the proud explosion of her people from the
concrete cages of America. We helped build this country.
We have paid our dues.

                        i'm
        gonna wear the robes and
        sit on the benches
        make the rules and make
        the arrests say
        who can and who
        can't
                        baby you don't stand
                        a
                        chance

        i'm

                gonna put black angels
                in all the books and a black
                Christchild in Mary's arms i'm
                gonna make black bunnies black
                fairies black santas black
                nursery rhymes and
                                black
                ice cream
                                i'm
        gonna make it a
                crime
                        to be anything BUT black

gonna make white
a twentyfourhour
lifetime
J.O.B.

Soul, then, is all of the unconscious energy of the Black
Experience. It is primal spiritual energy. One frequently
hears this expressed in terms like: "Soul is putting everything you have into it." "He sure got a whole lot of Soul in
it." "Soul is deep down feeling." With great perception,
William Melvin Kelley, in the June 1968 issue of *Jazz and
Pop* magazine described the modulations of James Brown's
voice as "the sounds of molecules cracking apart." Yet in
the same article the main point is that the French audience
for which James Brown is performing is disappointed because he is "not the Beatles." Still they have come to the
show to feed, so to speak, upon this energy, unaware that
they cannot handle it. And one recalls the early appear-
ances of James Brown on the "Ed Sullivan Show." For
about five minutes on one occasion Brown sings, dances,
preaches, croons, seduces, wails, makes love, and almost
drops from sheer exhaustion. The stunned white audience
responds with a polite patter of applause, unable to handle
all of that energy, all that love—survival motion set to
music. It overloaded their circuits, burnt them out!

I have called this energy spiritual, but really such a
designation is false, for it is physical as well, in fact, physical and spiritual at the same time, the expression of a
powerful total personality, drawing its reserve from centuries of suffering and joy compressed in the music of the
black Baptist church, lashing out in the dozens, flashing out
in the black lightning of the blues. Nor is the effect of this
expression altogether pleasant by Western standards, for

the rasp of the breath, the hoarseness of James Brown's
voice, somehow hurts our own throats, and despite the
incredible gracefulness of the intricate dances, we are painfully aware of the sheer physical drive involved in their
execution. And when James Brown is through with us,
when the Soul force is through with him, though completely exhausted, we feel curiously exalted.

Although the French audience that Kelley observed was
emotionally incapable of understanding Soul, the American
audience, even now, though not incapable of receiving the
emotional meaning of Soul, has a great deal of embarrassment with its other components. It seems a peculiarly
American thing, this embarrassment with the Black Experience of Soul because it lies close to the heart of the identity
problem of black and white alike. On one hand it is the
black bourgeois rejection of the folk culture; on the other it
is the perennial romance of the Noble Savage. One of the
most obvious forms that it has taken is the "minstrel" tradition, under which one can subsume a good deal of "American life," but for our purpose especially the history of jazz
and now the new rock music. We see it in ragtime, an early
white American music which, in effect, burlesqued black
music. We see it in the blackface minstrels. We see it in the
careers of Eddie Cantor and Al Jolson. We see it in the
early history of the movies. We still see it in the Sidney
Poitier phenomenon. We remember it from the
Amos'n'Andy shows, both radio and TV. And the Righteous Brothers, we remember again, were singing versions
of Amos'n'Andy, and Pat Boone told them so before a
nationwide audience. And one has only to mention the
early Beatles, the Rolling Stones, and the Animals. The fact
that they freely admitted their influences while Elvis Pres-
ley did not, alters the relationship only slightly. And, **of**

course, one could name many more examples. The important thing, however, is not the fact of the borrowing (or the stealing) but the attitude of the borrowers. The stance has been either condescending, or derogatory, or ironic. There were the coon lyrics of the ragtime songs and there are now the hyped-up names, many of which, as LeRoi Jones notes in *Black Music*,[32] are implicitly scornful of their sources. I can explain this only as a kind of perverse love: the love object must first be abused, then used. Strange Fruit! The source of the energy must be ridiculed, so that it can be exploited. In other words, Soul must be degraded so that it can be packaged. It must be reduced to "sound."

What has all of this to do with black writers and the black revolution? Everything. In the first place, what the black revolution seeks is not integration into American society as it now stands. A few years ago the slogan was, "Not integration but transformation." That, of course, is just a mild way of saying what has been said in other terms; and what has been said is that this society as we know it must be destroyed and another erected in its place. What has been said is that if we can't have our rightful place in this country, then we're gonna tear it up. What has been said is *Black Power!* which, curiously, has been embraced by everyone from Richard Nixon and Ralph McGill and Whitney Young to Julius Lester and Rap Brown and Stokeley Carmichael and Roy Innis.

What must be realized is that the distinction between Nixon's "black power" and Julius Lester's or that of the black man in the street is the awareness that white people can't give it to us, even if they wanted to, for underlying the political and social strategies of black power is the

32. New York: William Morrow, 1967.

spiritual energy of Soul. This is not the "Soul Force" which Dr. King named his newspaper after, though it is related to it, but the Will-to-Being, the Will-to-Blackness of a colonized people, conscious now of themselves in a way unprecedented in their history. The very concept of black power is informed with Soul, so on the deepest levels of meaning it implies a kind of society which is radically different from the one we now live in. It implies, to use Lerone Bennett's words again, a life geared to "the spirit rather than the letter, a relaxed and noncompetitive approach to being, a complex acceptance of the contradictions of life." It implies a society which "recognizes that machines are generative power and not soul, instruments and not ends."

Does America need such a society? Can it tolerate such a society? Over the past thirty years or so we have seen and heard a great deal about the abstraction of modern life, especially in the West. The late Professor J. P. Nettl of the University of Pennsylvania, writing in *The Nation*, attributed the decline of the intellectual to a "shift in consciousness; from a sense of common identity with a perceived whole idea to an impersonal bond tying individuals to an abstraction, membership in which has increasingly to be specified by laws and asserted by symbols like Thanksgiving Day or flag-waving week."[33] We know, all of us, how the "march of abstract modernity" has affected American life. We have all encountered the impersonality of institutions in every aspect of our lives—in the political, the religious, the academic, the social—and as a consequence we have all experienced the demeaning sense of powerless-

33. "Is the Intellectual Obsolete?" in *The Nation*, March 4, 1968, p. 302.

ness and invisibility that Ellison describes so well in *Invisible Man.*

Still the young and the black and the poor experience it with greater intensity and with a greater bitterness and frustration at our institutions and our national leaders. And their frustration—our frustration—has exploded all over this land: in Watts and in Berkeley, in Columbia and in Harlem, in Howard and in Newark, in Virginia Union and in Cleveland and Atlanta. Some concessions have been made; even more promises have been made and broken. The Poor People's Campaign has failed. The national circus continues. Most of the young get merely older and move to the suburbs, but an increasing number drop out altogether and form their own communities and profess the Soul life and call themselves the "new niggers." But the old niggers absorb niggerness into Soul knowing that they don't have the luxury of dropping back in again, knowing, in fact, that they were never really in. And this knowledge of having paid *real* dues provides a tragic dimension to black life in America that might finally serve to curb our national arrogance, to provide a sense of empathy with the "humiliated" peoples of the world whom we presume to lead and to defend.[34]

Dues must be paid. That is one of the chief lessons of the life of Soul, recorded in all of our literature and all of our song. As I see it, this awareness, splendid in its complex union with a seemingly inexhaustible energy, this way of life must be documented and articulated by our novelists and essayists and sung by our poets. It must be preserved and defended from commercial and political pollution, for the tools of "abstract modernity" are precise and precisely

34. See Vincent Harding, "The Uses of the Afro-American Past," in *Negro Digest,* Feb. 1968, pp. 83, 84.

dehumanizing. Finally, it is for black people, for Soul people, to realize the revolutionary potential in their way of
life, for Soul means wholeness and energy and healing. If
each of us became conscious of that potential, the United
States would either become whole itself or eradicate those
who tried to make it so. But a man who is whole does not
fear death. And so the final question is up to America: Can
you honestly accommodate this energy which you so vi-
tally need, or will your circuits, already overloaded, be
burnt out? Mari Evans, a proud black woman, says:

> baby you don't stand
> a
> chance
>
> . . . .
>
> i'm
> gonna make it a
>   crime
>   to be anything BUT black
>
> gonna make white
> a twentyfourhour
> lifetime
> J.O.B.

INDEX

Index

Wisconsin Books
on African and Afro-American Studies

ALAGOA, Ebiegberi Joe. *The Small Brave City-State: A History of Nembe-Brass in the Niger Delta.* 188 pages, 3 illus., 3 maps. $5.00.

COOK, Mercer and Stephen E. Henderson. *The Militant Black Writer in Africa and the United States.* 144 pages. Cloth $5.00; Paper $1.95.

CRONON, E. David. *Black Moses: The Story of Marcus Garvey and the Universal Negro Improvement Association.* Foreword by John Hope Franklin. 296 pages, 7 illus. Paper $1.95.

CURTIN, Philip D., ed. *Africa Remembered: Narratives by West Africans from the Era of the Slave Trade.* 376 pages, 20 illus., 16 maps. Cloth $10.00; Paper $2.95.

CURTIN, Philip D. *The Atlantic Slave Trade: A Census.* 312 pages. $7.50.

CURTIN, Philip D. *The Image of Africa: British Ideas and Action, 1780–1850.* 544 pages, 23 illus., 21 maps. $8.00.

FAGE, J. D. *Ghana: A Historical Interpretation.* Paul Knaplund Lectures in Commonwealth History, University of Wisconsin, 1956–57. Foreword by Philip D. Curtin. 128 pages, 2 maps. Paper $1.50.

GÉRARD-LIBOIS, Jules. *Katanga Secession.* Translated from the French by Rebecca Young. Originally published in 1963 as *Sécession au Katanga.* 338 pages, 3 maps. $8.50.

HARRIES, Lyndon, trans. and ed. *Poems from Kenya: Gnomic Verses in Swahili by Ahmad Nassir bin Juma Bhalo.* 264 pages. $5.00.

HUTCHISON, Thomas W., and others, eds. *Africa and Law: Developing Legal Systems in African Commonwealth Nations.* 200 pages. $6.50.

KOPYTOFF, Jean Herskovits. *A Preface to Modern Nigeria: The "Sierra Leonians" in Yoruba, 1830–1890.* 416 pages, 3 maps. $8.95.

LEWIS, Herbert S. *A Galla Monarchy: Jimma Abba Jifar, Ethiopia, 1830–1932.* 168 pages, 8 illus., 4 maps. $5.00.

MIRACLE, Marvin P. *Agriculture in the Congo Basin: Tradition and Change in African Rural Economies.* 372 pages, 20 figs., 23 maps. $8.50.

MIRACLE, Marvin P. *Maize in Tropical Africa.* 346 pages, 18 illus., 13 maps. $7.50.

ROUX, Edward. *Time Longer than Rope: A History of the Black Man's Struggle for Freedom in South Africa.* Foreword by Philip D. Curtin. (Revision of 1948 edition, with eight new chapters.) 488 pages. Cloth $6.50; Paper $2.95.

SIMOONS, Frederick J. *Northwest Ethiopia: Peoples and Economy.* 268 pages, 87 figs., 10 maps. $5.00.

SKINNER, Neil. *Hausa Readings: Selections from Edgar's Tatsuniyoyi.* 302 pages. $5.00.

VANSINA, Jan. *Kingdoms of the Savanna.* 374 pages, 14 maps. Paper $2.95.

Wisconsin Books
on American Literature

ADERMAN, Ralph M., ed. *The Letters of James Kirke Paulding.* 656 pages, 15 illus. $10.00.

BECK, Warren. *Man in Motion: Faulkner's Trilogy.* 216 pages. Paper $1.75.

FELTSKOG, E. N., ed. *Parkman, The Oregon Trail.* 854 pages, 77 illus., map. $15.00.

JACKSON, Esther Merle. *The Broken World of Tennessee Williams*. 208 pages, 5 illus. Cloth $5.75; Paper $1.75.

JONES, Howard Mumford. *History and the Contemporary: Essays in Nineteenth-Century Literature*. 184 pages. $4.50.

KAPLAN, Louis, compiler. *A Bibliography of American Autobiographies*. Prepared in association with James T. Cook, Clinton E. Colby, Jr., and Daniel C. Haskell. 384 pages. $6.00.

KARANIKAS, Alexander. *Tillers of a Myth: Southern Agrarians as Social and Literary Critics*. 264 pages. Cloth $6.50; Paper $2.50.

McDOWELL, Frederick P. W. *Ellen Glasgow and the Ironic Art of Fiction*. 304 pages. Paper $1.95.

POCHMANN, Henry A., general ed. *The Complete Works of Washington Irving. Journals and Notebooks, Volume I, 1803–1806*. Edited by Nathalia Wright. 768 pages, illus. $17.50.

POCHMANN, Henry A. *German Culture in America: Philosophical and Literary Influences, 1600–1900*. 880 pages. $7.50.

SEALTS, Merton M., Jr. *Melville's Reading: A Check-List of Books Owned and Borrowed*. 144 pages, 11 illus. $6.00.

Wisconsin Books
on Literary Criticism

CHARLESWORTH, Barbara. *Dark Passages: The Decadent Consciousness in Victorian Literature*. 172 pages. $5.00.

DEMBO, L. S., ed. *Criticism: Speculative and Analytical Essays*. Articles collected from the Summer 1968 issue of *Contemporary Literature*. 160 pages. Cloth $7.50; Paper $2.50.

DEMBO, L. S., ed. *Nabokov: The Man and His Work*. Articles collected from the Spring 1967 issue of *Wisconsin Studies in Contemporary Literature*, with the addition of two new articles. 290 pages. Cloth $6.50; Paper $2.50.

ENCK, John J. *Jonson and the Comic Truth*. 296 pages. Paper $1.95.

GREEN, Otis H. *Spain and the Western Tradition: The Castilian Mind in Literature from El Cid to Calderón*. Vol. I, 342 pages. Vol. II, 374 pages. Vol. III, 516 pages. Vol. IV, 356 pages. Vols. I, II, and IV, Cloth $7.50; Paper $2.95. Vol III, Cloth $10.00; Paper $2.95.

HERRIOTT, J. Homer. *Toward a Critical Edition of the Celestina*. 304 pages, 253 graphs. $10.00.

KIELL, Norman, compiler and ed. *Psychoanalysis, Psychology, and Literature: A Bibliography*. 232 pages. $5.00.

KROEBER, Karl. *The Artifice of Reality: Poetic Style in Wordsworth, Foscolo, Keats, and Leopardi*. 256 pages. $6.50.

KROEBER, Karl. *Romantic Narrative Art*. 238 pages. Paper $1.95.

LOFTUS, Richard J. *Nationalism in Modern Anglo-Irish Poetry*. 374 pages. $6.50.

MILOSH, Joseph E. *The Scale of Perfection and the English Mystical Tradition*. 226 pages. $6.50.

ORNSTEIN, Robert. *The Moral Vision of Jacobean Tragedy*. 310 pages. Paper $2.25.

ROSSI, Joseph, and Alfred Galpin, eds. and trans. *De Sanctis on Dante*. 192 pages. $4.00.

RUGGIERS, Paul G. *The Art of the Canterbury Tales*. 284 pages. Cloth $6.00; Paper $2.95.

WEBBER, Joan. Contrary Music: The Prose of John Donne. 240 pages. $5.50.

WEBBER, Joan. *The Eloquent "I": Style and Self in Seventeenth-Century Prose*. 312 pages, 2 illus. $8.50.

WILKIE, Brian. *Romantic Poets and Epic Tradition*. 288 pages. $6.50.

YOUNG, Howard T. *The Victorious Expression: A Study of Four Contemporary Spanish Poets, Unamuno, Machado, Jiménez, and Lorca*. 248 pages. Cloth $6.50; Paper $1.95.

GREENVILLE COLLEGE LIBRARY

896C77   C001
COOK, MERCER, 1903-
THE MILITANT BLACK WRITER IN AFRIC STX

3 4511 00082 5071

DATE DUE

GAYLORD   PRINTED IN U.S.A